AF656087

INDIA'S QUEST FOR PERMANENT SEAT IN UNSC:
CHALLENGES AND PROSPECTS

INDIA'S QUEST FOR PERMANENT SEAT IN UNSC:
CHALLENGES AND PROSPECTS

Shriya Mokta

CRESCENT
PUBLISHING CORPORATION

India's Quest for Permanent Seat in UNSC: Challenges and Prospects

© Shriya Mokta

Edition 2026

ISBN 978-81-949754-4-1

Published by:
CRESCENT PUBLISHING CORPORATION
4806/24, Mathur Lane,
Ansari Road, Darya Ganj,
New Delhi - 110 002
Ph.: 011 - 23244131
Mob.: + 91 - 9711991838, 9999021668
E-mail: crescentbook@gmail.com
Website: www.crescentpublishingcorp.weebly.com

PRINTED IN INDIA

Preface

United Nations Organization is an International Organization, which was established in 1945. The UN as an Organisation is the only hope for nation of the world to live in peace and dignity, to share wealth and assets of the planet without exploiting them, to eradicate disease, hunger, exploitation, and above all to retain and nurture their unique "Nationhood".

Reforms and reorganization of structure and processes of the Security Council are urgently required to regain its lost credibility. The membership of the Security Council has changed very little since its inception in 1945, even though the number of UN member states has almost quadrupled since then and the relative power of member states has changed significantly. Addition of four non-permanent seats in 1965 was the only change in membership made. African states call the under-representation of Africa as historical injustice.

Performance of the Security Council in maintaining international peace and security has been poor. No feature of United Nations activity has raised more doubts about the ability of international organizations to assure peace and security than the frequent use of veto by United Nations Security Council. On many occasion the P5 have abused their veto power.

India was also elected as non-permanent member of Security Council eight times. India has a strong claim for permanent membership of Security Council. India claim its membership as permanent member of Security Council as India is second largest country in terms of population, with one of the world's largest economies and the third largest contributor of troops to UN peace-keeping missions. This book makes an attempt to strengthen India's claim and will also be helpful to students of International Relations to analyse and understand India's claim for permanent membership of Security Council. When India's eighth tenure as non-permanent member of Security Council started from January 1, 2021 and India is pursuing hard for permanent membership of Security Council, India captured international attention and enhanced the image of India with a profound change. India is being viewed as a major pole in the configuration of the emerging global balance of power by outsiders as well as Indians themselves. On the basis of its population, territorial size, GDP, economic potential, civilization legacy, cultural diversity, political system and past and on-going contributions to the activities of the UN, especially to UN peacekeeping operations, India is eminently qualified for permanent membership.

Present Book is in Five Chapters. First Chapter gives introduction about the Security Council. Second Chapter highlights Organization set up and functions of Security Council. Third chapter throws light on reforms in Security Council. Fourth Chapter discusses India's claim for Permanent seat in Security Council. Last Fifth Chapter highlights concluding remarks.

For inclusion in the permanent membership seat of Security Council, Indian tryst for permanent membership of Security Council is justified. As an undisputed leader of the Third World countries, India has been acknowledged as a rising power by the world. Time has come when the Security Council has to grow out of its five power mind-set to survive. India has to display more pragmatism to realize its aspiration to be a permanent member of the Security Council.

This Book is of immense value for researchers,students and others studying foreign policy and international relations.

Shriya Mokta

..

Contents

List of Abbreviations

Art.	Article
COP	Conference of Parties
CTBT	Comprehensive Test Ban Treaty
G77	Group of 77
GNP	Gross National Product
IAEA	International Atomic Energy Agency
ICC	International Criminal Court
ICJ	International Court of Justice
IGO	Inter Governmental Organisation
IPKF	Indian Peace Keeping Forces
ISA	International Solar Alliance
L-69	42-member grouping of developing countries from Asia, Africa and Latin America
NAM	Non Aligned Movement
NPT	Non Proliferation Treaty
NSG	Nuclear Supplier Group
NSG	Nuclear Suppliers Group
P5	Permanent 5

R2P	Responsibility to Protect
RUF	Revolutionary United Front
RUF	Revolutionary United Front
SC	Security Council
UN	United Nations
UNAMIR	United Nations Assistance Mission in Rwanda
UNAMSIL	United Nations Mission in Sierra Leone
UNAVEM	United Nations Angola Verification Mission
UNEF	United Nations Emergency Force
UNESCO	United Nations Educational, Scientific and Cultural Organisation
UNGA	United Nations General Assembly
UNICEF	United Nation Children Fund
UNIFIL	United Nations Interim Force in Lebanon
UNITA	National Union for the Total Independence of Angola
UNMIK	United Nations Peacekeeping Mission in Kosovo
UNMIL	United Nations Mission in Liberia
UNTAC	United Nations Transitional Authority in Cambodia
UNTAG	United Nations Transition Assistance Group

Chapter - 1

Introduction

The United Nations came into being at a historic conjunction marking termination of the era of the "old new world" (Ramcharit, 1998).The United Nations has been the most institutionalized expression to date of the international concern for colonial peoples (Singh, 1986). Since World War II the United Nations has been the central piece of Global governance. It is the only Inter Government Organisation (IGO) with Global scope and nearly universal membership whose agenda encompasses the broadest range of governance. Reforms and reorganizations of its structures and operational system have been a continuous process from the very inception(Saksena,1946).The present form of the United Nations has history of millennium and the traces can be found way back in "The Amplietyonic League of Greeks" of the 6th B.C. The league was formed with the objective of creating international unity and avoiding war. Thereafter the Confederation Delos was formed in 477 B.C. by the member states of the shores, Trace and Propionates provided a common Navy by making contributions of ships and men. In the process another confederation was formed by the Greek known as the Achaean League of Hellenise. The outside nations were not admitted as members. The league had about seventeen member states.

International Organizations are the most well equipped institutions to cope with international problems (Sud, 1983).The Romans also contributed a lot to the growth of international organisation by giving an idea of legal, military and administrative techniques. In 1305 A.D. a plan was proposed for an alliance of the Christian Powers by Pierre

Qubies, a French lawyer. He pleaded for the establishment of a Permanent Court of Arbitration for the settlement of disputes among the members of alliance, although it failed, being defective for want of adequate machinery for interstate co-operation.

Another league known as the Hanseatic League was formed in 1315 for the promotion of trade. In the process many important steps in development and establishment of international organisations have taken place in the past such as the Grand Design 1603 and the Peace Treaty of Westphalia in 1648.

Another treaty known as the Peace of Utrecht 1713 furthered the creation of several sovereignties. The international peace conferences held at Hague in 1899 and 1907 were notable as major diplomatic gatherings in time of peace with the involvement of a variety of subjects like the business of international relations, law of sea, sea trade and territorial matter.

League of Nations

The First World War (1914-1918) jolted the political conscience of the world governments. After the outbreak of world war, an important international organization took birth known as League of Nations. The League of Nations Covenant was part of the peace treaties drawn up by the victorious Allied and Associated Powers at the end of the war of 1914-1918 and imposed on the central power(Samarsen,1996).It proved causes of emergence in brief –organisation and funding and proved helpful in the furtherance of co-operation in economic and social matters like health, traffic in opium, communication and to transmit economic and financial problems protection of refugees, trafficking of women and children etc.

The Failure of the League of Nations

The League of Nations did not fail because of its principles and conceptions. It failed because these principles were deserted by those states which has brought it into being(Sharma,1978).The League of Nations failed due to the split between Great Britain and France, the failure of United States to ratify and there by become a member. Actually, United States contributed to the downfall of the league from the outside and many of its members from the inside. Moreover, the league failed to prevent the Second World War and to promote peace. Therefore the people all over the world were looking for another effective system of collective security (Geneva, 1940).

Atlantic Charter (1941)

On August 11, 1941 President Roosevelt (USA) and Prime Minister Churchill signed a joint declaration called the Atlantic Charter that assumed that victors in the war will have to police international scene for maintaining peace in the future.

The Casablanca Conference (Jan. 1943)

In January 1943, Prime Minister Churchill and President Roosevelt met the French representative in the city of Casablanca in North Africa to plan invasion of Italy and Sicily. They agreed on a formula of unconditional surrender talked over the terms of peace.

The Food and Agriculture Conference (May-June-1943)

In 1943, the Food and Agriculture conference was held at Hot Springs, Virginia, which was attended by the representatives of forty four nations. The conference studied the problems of feeding millions of displaced persons and laid the ground work for the activities which led to the establishment of the Food and Agriculture Organization in late 1945.

The Moscow Declaration (Oct. 30-1943)

The Moscow Declaration of October 30, 1943 signed by Molotov for the Soviet Union, Eden for Great Britain, Hull for the United States signed for China, was probably one of the important steps in the direction of forming the United Nations (U.N.). By this declaration the four Great, powers declared that they recognize the 'necessity of establishing at the earliest practical date a general International Organization, based on the principle of sovereign, equality of all peace loving states and open to membership by all such states, large; and small, for the maintenance of international peace and security.

The Tehran Conferences (Nov. 1943)

President Roosevelt, Prime Minister Churchill and Premier Stalin met at Tehran and issued a joint statement on Dec. 1, 1943, by which they accepted the supreme responsibility to make peace which will command the goodwill of the overwhelming masses of the people of the world and banish the scourge and terror of war for many generations.

The Breton Woods Conference (July, 1944)

The representatives of forty four nations, acting on the assumption that no peace could last if economic and financial chaos prevailed, met at San Francisco and drew up an agreement by which The International Bank for Reconstruction and Development (IBRD) and The International Monetary Fund were established. Both these agencies are now actively functioning as specialized agencies of the' United Nations.

The Dumbarton Oaks Conference (Aug-Oct 1944)

The Oaks Conference held at Washington from Aug 21, 1944 to Oct. 7, 1944 was the next major step in the development of the United Nations Charter. The proceedings of the conference can broadly be divided into two phases. In the first phase, representatives of United States/the United Kingdom and the Soviet Union conferred premix weeks on the main outlines, of the proposer international organization. In the second phase the representatives of the Soviet Union were dropped and replaced by those of China. The proposals for the establishment of a general International Organization were published on Oct. 9, 1944 and were sent to all the other United Nations governments for review. These proposals can very well be considered the first draft of the United Nations charter. However, they were briefer than the final charter, particularly in respect to economic and functional organization.

Crimea Conference (1945)

In Feb, 1945 voting procedure was discussed at the Crimea Conference in 1945 according to the formulae presented by President Roosevelt.

The Yalta Conference (Feb. 1945)

The question of voting procedure in the Security Council which remained unsolved at Dumbarton Oaks was taken up at the Yalta conference held in February, 1945 and was discussed there by President Roosevelt, Prime Minister Churchill, and Marshal Stalin. These powers also drafted plans for the occupation and control of defeated Germany and for keeping order in liberated Europe. The veto formula later embodied in the U.N. charter was also finalized at the Yalta Conference. Finally it was decided to hold a full scale United Nations conference to convene in San Francisco on April 25, 1945.

Committee of Jurist's Meeting (April-1945)

The Jurists from forty four nations met at Washington and drew up a draft statute and report, which with certain amendments was adopted as the statute of the International Court of Justice. United States President Franklin D. Roosevelt coined the term "United Nations". It was used first time in the Declaration by United Nations of 1 January 1942 when 26 nations' representatives pledged to continue fighting against Axis Powers during the Second World War.

The San Francisco Conference (April-June 26, 1945)

The San Francisco Conference produced a consensus among its participants at least on one point :the necessity of creating an effective security system (Saksena, 1974).The Charter of the United Nations, signed at San Francisco on June 26,1945 by the representatives of fifty nations, was the product of an evolutionary development extending over a period of many decades even centuries (Goodrich,1946).Fifty governments met in San Francisco on 25 April 1945 started drafting the UN charter which was later on adopted on 25 June 1945. The charter came into effect on 24 October 1945.

Birth of the United Nations (October 24, 1945)

So many efforts and steps were taken by the world community from 1941 to 1945. The United Nations as a global diplomatic and political organization arose on the ashes of the League of Nations that was created by the Treaty of Versailles in 1919 and disbanded in 1946. It was second multipurpose international organization established in the 20th century.

The United Nations charter was signed on June 26, 1945 in San Francisco at the conclusion of United Nations Conference on International Organization. The charter came into force on Oct. 24, 1945 by which time China, France, Russia, the United Kingdom, the United States and a majority of the other signatories had ratified the document. It was launched on the perilous international seas on January 10, 1946, when the first session of the General Assembly commenced in London. It consists the Preamble and 19 chapters divided into 111 articles.

Purpose and Principles of the United Nations

Purpose and Principles of UN are outlined in Articles 1 and 2 of the charter of the United Nations

Article 1(2) Equal Rights and determination of people

Article 2(4) Prohibition of threat or use of force in international relations

Article 2(5) Obligation to give assistance to United Nations and refrain from assisting states targets with preventive or enforcement actions

Article 2(6) Need to ensure that non United Nations Members act in accordance with its principles

Article 2(7) Non-intervention in domestic affairs by the United Nations.

United Nations worked on three pillars - peace and security, human rights and development. The six main organs of United Nations are General Assembly, the Security Council, The Economic and Social Council, The Trusteeship Council, the International Court of Justice and the UN secretariat all established in 1945. Initially UN had only 51 members with the addition of South Sudan in 2011 its membership increased to 193. Thus, there are 193 members in United Nations, plus two non-member countries with permanent observer states, The Vatican and the State of Palestine

Graph 1.1: Growth of UN Membership (1945-2020)

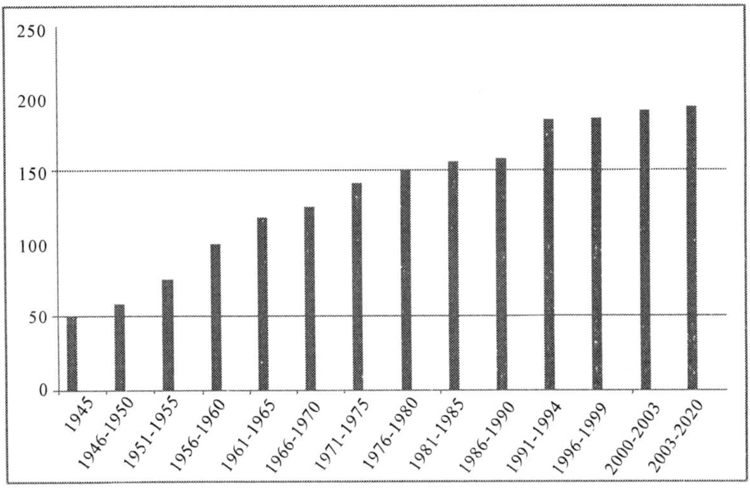

Source: www.un.org

Its core values are integrity, professionalism and respect for diversity. Six official languages of United Nations are Arabic, Chinese, English, French, and Russian and Spanish. In UN system various specialised agencies, funds and programmes like World Bank Group, World Health Organization, World Food Programme, and UNESCO and UNICEF are there. Secretary General of United Nations is Antonio Guterres from Portuguese, who began his five year term from 1 January, 2017.

Graph 1.2: Contributors to UN Regular Budget (2019-2021)

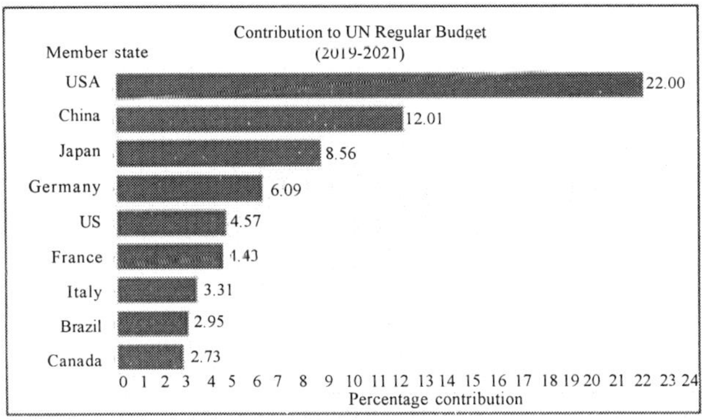

Source: www.un.org

It is evident from the analysis of the above graph that USA's GNP in 2018 was approximately 24 percent of the total GNP of all the member countries of the UN and thus its highest share of contribution was from USA. China contributes the second highest with 12.05 percent, followed by Japan (8.56 percent), Germany (6.09percent), United Kingdom of Great Britain and North Ireland (4.56percent) and France (4.43percent) in the top five after USA. Italy has surpassed Brazil (2.93 percent) in the list to become the seventh largest contributor (3.31percent).Eighteen countries contribute more than 1percent each to the UN regular budget. 175 countries contribute less than 0.1percent each including India's neighbours Pakistan, Bangladesh and Nepal.

As the intergovernmental structure grew and its activities widened, the UN had to grapple with endemic institutional problems relating to effectiveness and efficacy.

Security Council

The creation of Security Council within the scheme of international organizations is the result of development of powerful states within the world community and their desire to control the affairs of the world in their own fashion (Webster, 1933). The nation states as their emergence on the world scene were in a sense as much in a state of nature towards each other as human communities at the dawn of history. Nevertheless, the technique of diplomacy had been changed from bilateral to multilateral (Mangone, 1954).

United Nations Security Council was set up to maintain international peace and security in accordance with the principles of the United Nations: Security Council investigates any dispute or situation which might lead to the disturbance of peace and causes international friction. It recommends methods of the adjusting such disputes or the terms of settlement. On the one hand Security council formulates plans for the establishment of a system to regulate armaments; In order to function effectively Security council has been authorised to call on Members to apply economic sanctions and other measures not involving the use of force to prevent or stop aggression; in this context Security council can take military action against an aggressor. Along with this Security Council recommend the admission of new Members; and exercise the trusteeship functions of the United Nations in "strategic areas. The Security Council recommends the General Assembly regarding appointment of the Secretary-General, together with the General Assembly elects the judges of International Court of justice (http://www.un.org).

Need for Reforms in Security Council

In order to meet the realities of the 21st Century, an urgent need of reforms in United Nations Security Council has been felt for a long time. No reforms of United Nations are complete without changing the composition of the Security Council (Nafed, 2005).

United Nations Security Council was established by 51 countries 75 years ago in 1945 and the UN now has 193 member states that coexist but it is still running on the same wheels. When the world is facing threat of Global peace and security the need for effective Security Council is needed. When there is transition of unipolar world to multipolar world, there is threefold increase in global population, threats of terrorism and cybercrime are challenging world peace, security, national stability and World is rapidly changing. It is very unfortunate with changing pace of the world United Nations Security Council (UNSC) is not changing. To reform the UNSC without amending the UN Charter is a difficult task. In accordance with Article 109 of the UN Charter, a simple majority of members of the UN General Assembly (currently 97 out of 193 members) and a vote by any seven members of the UNSC, for a General Conference of UN member states is required to amend the UN Charter. The amendment would subsequently need to be ratified by national legislatures as set out in the Charter (Cilliers, 2015). Today the world is passing through a difficult phase. In a cold war situation after pandemic the world is again on the verge of war. The Security Council permanent membership needs reformation at this crucial stage (Joshi, 2020).

India's Claim for Permanent membership of Security Council

By all reckoning, India has arrived on the world stage. India's large and rapidly expanding economy coupled with its huge population and nuclear power captured international attention and enhanced the image of India with a profound change. India is being viewed as a major pole in the configuration of the emerging global balance of power by outsiders as well as Indians themselves (Pant, 2009).

India hopes that its continued leadership of various Global South forums such as G 77 and NAM would garner much needed numbers in the UNGA. This is reflected in India's strong defence of the principle of sovereignty and the constant voluble criticism of the "Responsibility to Protect."

On the other hand, India's growing strategic partnerships with the P5, including the historic nuclear deal with the US in 2005, reiteration of historic ties with Russia, paint a favourable picture for Indian hopes in the Security Council by the existing permanent members.

Prime Minister Modi reiterated that the UNSC "must include the world's largest democracies, major locomotives of the global economy, and voices from all major continents" to carry "greater credibility and legitimacy." Making a much stronger case for the G4 in its entirety, he said that "more Member States have the capacity and willingness to take on major responsibilities with regard to maintenance of international peace and security." Further, with India as part of G4, it seems to have limited its options to negotiate a seat for it as a great power and regional politics would circumscribe the G4 attempts to win permanent seats for all as a group (General, 2017).

India has also joined the L-69, the 42-member grouping of developing countries from Asia, Africa and Latin America. India also, in late 2016, joined as a member the newly founded group of friends on UN Security Council Reform, created to accelerate the negotiating process of Council reforms. India's relations with contiguous neighbours, extended neighbours, major global powers and regional organisations have been considerably improved with the solidarity exception of Pakistan and China (Singh, 2017).

India has been acknowledged as a rising power by most of the states. Also, there is a pressing need to democratize multilateral forum, starting from the United Nations system itself. In this context, India is making a legitimate claim for its rightful place in the changing architecture of global governance, including the UN Security Council(Indian Express, 2020).Time has come when India must think to take a step towards a non-permanent seat on the UNSC (UNSC, 2019).

Review of Literature

Batra (1979) presents a historical analysis of the Growth of State System and war. His book discusses Security Council of the United Nations Organizations and discusses in detail veto power exercised by Security Council, its use and abuse.

Maaroof (1990) in his book presents of an inside and out assessment about the role of Afghanistan in strengthening the United Nations from September 1946 when it joined the advent of communist coup in Kabul in April 1978. The book also deals with the emergence of the question of Afghanistan before the Security Council their before the general assembly.

Sen (1996) in his volume *UN and the Global Challenge* attempts to bring together select readings on power politics in the context of nations and the wider context of the country of nations under the auspices of the United Nations. The Book discusses in detail about the role and functions of Security Council and discusses survival or success of International Organizations.

Herzog (1999) argues that globalization entails a certain loss of sovereignty, as certain parameters of economic policy making are governed by international agreements and are thus removed from further democratic discussion. Moreover, it becomes difficult to sustain economic policies that are disliked by the markets, especially the capital markets, such as large fiscal deficits, high inflation, unrealistic and volatile exchange rates. Weaknesses in financial systems are exposed faster and have grave consequences.

Kapstein (2000) formulates a relevant question in this regard: "Is globalization responsible for the growing polarity in wages now being observed in many countries around the world, creating a sharp divide between society's 'winners' and 'losers'?...If not globalization, what is responsible for that trend, and what, if anything, should policy makers do in response?" There seems to be a widespread view among economists that globalization has resulted in unskilled workers becoming particularly vulnerable to economic and technological change and they seem to be falling behind their more highly educated colleagues in terms of earnings and job security.

Bhola (2001) Author throws light that India and China are considered two major constituents of this power centre but much will depend upon cooperation, confrontation and engagement between these two countries. Tension and conflict between these countries can be properly understood on the basis of Foreign policies of these two countries

Duane (2002) brings political interests and institutions – centre stage to argue that democratic processes and national institutions are fundamentally important to determining how internationalization affects domestic policy change. Swank documents a number of rollbacks in benefit levels and restrictions in eligibility, cost controls and privatizations of social services, and related neo-liberal policies across the developed capitalist democracies. But he suggests that there is no evidence that these policy changes have been driven directly and systematically by globalization in the developed democracies as a whole, or in the largest welfare states. His work encapsulates an impressive number of case studies of developed welfare states on both sides of the Atlantic.

Bilgrami (2004) throws light on dynamic of sanctions in World Affairs. It discusses in detail about theories of sanction and its effect of UN sanctions on Iran and Iraq.

Wet (2004) in his book gives an exhaustive examination of the inquiries relating to the forces of the Security Council under Chapter VII of the Charter of the United Nations. In doing as such it leaves from the reason that an examination of the restrictions to the forces of the Security Council and an investigation of legal survey of such constraints by the ICJ, individually, are between ward. From one viewpoint, legal audit would possibly end up applicable if and to the degree that the forces allowed to the Security Council under Chapter VII of the Charter are liable to justifiable confinements.

Sinha (2004) provides insight into social economic and political stability in India 2025.The dawn of new millennium provides the opportunity for fresh assessment about the progress made by India so far and for identifying the likely parameters of the country, social economic and political stability in the year to come.

Luck (2006) looks at the antecedents of the UN Security Council, as well as the current issues and future challenges that it faces. this work includes, historical perspectives, the founding vision, procedures and practices, economic enforcement, peace operations and military enforcement, human security, proliferation and WMD, terrorism and reform, adaptation and change in respect of the international system and the United Nations.

Allain (2008) in his work referenced that the Slavery has taken on included hugeness in the twenty-first century because of its consideration in the Statute of the International Criminal Court and it being a segment some portion of the 2001 UN and 2005 Council of Europe traditions against dealing. With restricted and clashing case-law on the issue, the incorporating of the Travaux PrA (c) paratoires of the 1926 League of Nations and the 1956 United Nations traditions become fundamental in looking to considering States or people in charge of infringement of worldwide law addressing subjection. The Travaux PrA (c) paratoires of the bondage traditions give experiences into the meanings of subjugation, the slave exchange, and different sorts of servile statuses while uncovering data with respect to the different commitments that States have attempted to stifle the different signs of human misuse.

Boulden, Thakur, Weiss (2009) in their book looks at UN on-screen characters, apparatuses, and issues related with the changing idea of the earth in which it works; the manners by which it has and may react to innovative and political issues; and the inquiries and troubles that emerge for the world association. Issues canvassed in the book incorporate doctrinal inquiries on the utilization of power, the provincial elements of atomic multiplication, and developing worry that the atomic request built up by the Nuclear Non-expansion Treaty may crumple or essentially be surpassed by occasions. The United Nations and Nuclear

Orders fills this void by revealing insight into the past, present, and future jobs of the UN in reacting to the dangers and difficulties presented by atomic weapons.

Aslund, Guriev, Kuchins (2010) in their edited volume analyzed the imperative nation after the monetary emergency of 2007– 09. The Russia Balance Sheet Project, overwhelming exploration organizations, the Peterson Institute for International Economics and the Centre for Strategic and International Studies (CSIS), not just evaluates Russia and global and household approach difficulties yet additionally gives a widely inclusive audit of this vital nation and remote and local issues.

Lowe, Welsh (2010) in their work expressed around an initial diagram of the Council, it's developing jobs and obligations. This is the principal significant investigation of the United Nations Security Council part in tending to the issue of war, both common and worldwide, since 1945. "Both amid and after the Cold War the Council has acted in a constrained and specific way, and its work has once in a while brought about disappointment. It has not been and was never prepared to be the focal point of a thorough arrangement of aggregate security. Be that as it may, it remains the body accused of essential obligation regarding universal peace and security. It offers one of kind open doors for universal meeting and military joint effort, and for creating legitimate and regulating structures. It has had an impact in the decrease in the occurrence of worldwide war in the period since 1945. The United Nations Security Council and War inspects the degree to which crafted by the UN Security Council, as it has advanced, has or has not supplanted more seasoned frameworks of intensity governmental issues and works on with respect to the utilization of power.

Hening (2010) in his book expressed that the worldwide condition of 1919-1920 and the effect that of the principal World War was extensive and durable; a great part of the harm was promptly unmistakable, for example, the abrupt end of four extraordinary realms, gigantic budgetary obligation among countries, the episode of upheavals and of genuine social turmoil in Europe as well as over the globe, and not least the undeniable physical harm in the state of the scarred battlegrounds and crushed locales of France and Belgium. It was basic that a League of Nations was built as fast as could be expected under the circumstances. Its foundation would be one of only a handful couple of substantial increases of the war, filling in as an image of trust in missions of deprived families, uprooted the penance had not been futile, and that the finish of the First World War would genuinely achieve enduring harmony among countries.

Mallam (2012) reflects a debate of divergent views of states on the reform of the UN system generally and specifically, the UNSC. Basically, two groups form this debate: states who want minimal reforms and states who want broad reforms in the UNSC. The second group thus suggest geographical representation which would make room for a balanced UNSC thereby securing the peace of the globe. This is because regions of the world such as Africa, Asia, Latin America and eastern Europe which are prone to more threats of insecurity and by extension pose as threats to international peace and security are unrepresented. There is no doubt that the UN could benefit from some serious reforms however, one of the major ones would be an exclusion of the influence of individual member states other than when expressed in collective decisions by bodies such as the GA, and the SC. The strength of the UN is that it includes every state within a common umbrella. Since the UN in the view of this book is essential to world peace and security, it should be built up and not torn down.

Mukherjee (2013) provides historical overview of India's relationship with UNSC. This article throws light on contemporary constraints on India's ability to exercise greater influence at the UN. The concluding section sketches what an alternative Indian policy at the UN could look like.

Genser, Ugarte (2014) in their book analyses questions, for example, "How is the Security Council managing human rights concerns? What does it see as the spot of human rights in struggle avoidance, harmony making, and peacekeeping? Also, how can it address the mission for equity even with gross infringement of human rights? The United Nations Security Council in the age of Human Rights is the primary thorough take a gander at the human-rights measurements of crafted by the main body inside the United Nations framework equipped for convincing activity by its part states. Known prevalently for its inability to counteract mass monstrosities in Rwanda, the previous Yugoslavia, and Syria, the broadness and profundity of the Security Council and work on human rights in on-going decades is a lot more extensive".

Korbel (2015) in his work gives an incredible introduction of the numerous perplexing elements which originate from the Kashmir debate among India and Pakistan. The creator as the first Czech individual from the United Nations Commission for India and Pakistan, conveys to his story direct understanding.

Hayes, Yi (2015) in his volume recognizes key weight focuses at which common society can push for productive changes particularly ones that diminish the North Korean danger to its neighbours. Uncommonly, this book is both hypothetical and handy. Intricacy, Security and Civil Society in East Asia presents methodologies that can be driven by common society and consulted by its ambassadors to acknowledge peace, security, and supportability around the world. This volume is an absolute necessity perused for negotiators, researchers, understudies, columnists, activists, and individual peruses looking for knowledge into how to unravel the critical issues within recent memory. Multifaceted nature, Security and Civil Society in East Asia offers the most recent comprehension of complex worldwide issues in the locale, including atomic weapons, urban weakness, vitality, and environmental change. Point by point contextual analyses of China, North and South Korea, and Japan show the significance of common society and urban tact in achieving shared answers for these issues in East Asia and past. Every section depicts provincial common society activities that handle complex difficulties to East Asia security.

Nadin (2016) comprehensively evaluates the current state and future reform prospects of the UN Security Council, providing the most accessible and rigorous treatment of the subject of reform to date. Apart from a couple of critical eyes in the academic community, few have asked the pertinent questions that this volume seeks to address: Will the enlargement of the Council constitute a reform? Could the inclusion of countries such as India, Germany, Japan, and Brazil markedly improve the Council's agency?

Singh (2017) explores the initiatives taken by Prime Minister Modi. India strengthened its relation with nations in the region and beyond while taking the leap of stepping up relations with nations on to the next stage of partnership and cooperation.

Menon (2020) India finds itself in an increasingly dangerous world, one that is fragmenting and slowing down economically. It is a world in transition, one in which India's adversaries state or non-state, or both as in Pakistan's case — are becoming increasingly powerful. If the external world is becoming more unpredictable and uncertain, so are internal politics and security in most of the powers. These are challenges that traditional institutions and state structures are not well-equipped to handle, mitigate, or solve.

Davydov (2020) The article talks about recent events in relations between the PRC, the USA and Russia, the "Big Three" countries participating in the struggle for the formation of a new world order, their role and opportunities in this process in the context of the outbreak of the global coronary virus pandemic and the prospects for the development of relations between them in the foreseeable future. The author focuses on his conclusions made taking into account the features of the current moment.

Pal and Bansal (2020) discusses the outbreak of the novel Corona virus has been stated as a pandemic by World Health Organisation The World Health Organisation enunciates to all of the countries in the world to continue efforts that have been effective in limiting the number of cases and slow down the spread of the virus social distancing has been addressed as the most effective measure of mitigation This study highlights the impact of lockdown on pollution level along with a suggestion to the government to implement a one day lockdown in 3-4 months to put a check on pollution Mother Nature is expecting from us through present crisis to reciprocate perfectively and positively.

Selection of the Problem: United Nations Organization is an international Organization, which was established in 1945. Currently it has 193 member states and two observer states. No feature of United Nations activity has raised more doubts about the ability of international organizations to assure peace and security than the frequent use of veto by United Nations (Padelford, 1948). On many occasion The P5 have abused their veto power. In total 263 vetoes have been exercised since 1946, the year after the UN charter was officially ratified Performance of the Security Council in maintaining international peace and security has been poor. The membership of the Security Council has changed very little since its inception in 1945, even though the number of UN member states has almost quadrupled since then and the relative power of member states has changed significantly. Addition of four non-permanent seats in 1965 was the only change in membership made. African states call the under-representation of Africa as Historical injustice. New permanent member can be added to Security Council only through an amendment of Chapter 18 of UN Charter. Germany, Japan, India and Brazil (known later as the Group of Four or G4) formed in 2005 is political cooperative alliance and support each other bid for permanent membership of Security Council.

India claim its membership as permanent member of Security Council as India is second largest country in terms of population, with one of the world's largest economies and the third largest contributor of troops to UN peace-keeping missions. When India's eighth tenure as non-permanent member of Security Council starting from January 1, 2021and India is pursuing hard for permanent membership of Security Council, this topic assumes importance and is selected for study. Moreover because of the personal interest of researcher in International affairs this topic is selected for study.

Importance of Study

The UN as an Organisation is the only hope for nation of the world to live in peace and dignity, to share wealth and assets of the planet without exploiting them, to eradicate disease, hunger, exploitation, and above all to retain and nurture their unique "nationhood". Since its beginning in 1946, The United Nation Security Council has undergone reforms only once in 1963 when United Nations member states voted to expand UNSC from 11 to 15 members. In order to ensure universal implementation of decisions pertaining to peace building and non-proliferation there is urgent need for reforms in Security Council. India was sole candidate from Asia Pacific region vying for non-permanent membership and its candidature was unanimously endorsed by the 55 members of Asia Pacific group. India was also elected as non-permanent member of Security council eight times, keeping these aspects into consideration India has a strong claim for permanent membership of Security Council. Keeping these aspects into consideration present study assumes importance. Findings of the research will be helpful to strengthen India's claim and will also be helpful to students of International Relations to analyse and understand India's claim for permanent membership of Security Council.

Objectives of the Study

1. Study the history and growth of United Nations.
2. To understand the role of International Organizations in World Politics.
3. To examine the organisational setup and the functioning of Security Council.
4. Critically assess the different reform proposals regarding the UNSC.
5. To examine the Indian role in UN and UNSC and explore future possibilities of its claim to permanent membership.
6. To study the major challenges before Indian claim to UNSC permanent membership and underline the future prospects.

Research Methodology

The present study is based on qualitative research methodology. The study is based on historical, analytical and descriptive methods which included the use of primary and secondary sources. A large number books articles and journals have been consulted as the secondary sources. Background information regarding the working of council has been retrieved from the Repertoire of the Practice of Security Council as well as from the Repertory of Practice of United Nations Organs. Tables, graphs and charts have been used in research to analyse functioning of Security Council

For conducting research two basic approaches have been adopted. First, an initial review of literature on the Security Council has been done in general and in particular its work has been analysed. In understanding the claim for India on permanent membership of Security Council various aspects relating to India's emerging potential were taken into consideration. In Covid-19 pandemic situation how the claim of India for permanent membership of Security Council was strengthened has also been discussed and analysed.

Chapterization

1) Introduction
2) UNSC: Organizational Set up and Functions
3) Reforms in Security Council
4) India's Claim for Permanent Membership in UNSC
5) Conclusions and Suggestions.

References

Abbi, R. (2017). *United Nations Organization:Its Role in Third World Countries.* New Delhi: The Readers Paradise.

Allain, Jean (2008). *The Slavery Conventions: The Travaux Préparatoires of the 1926 League of Nations Convention and the 1956 United Nations Convention.* USA: Martinus Nijhoff Publishers.

Aslund, Anders, Sergei Guriev, Andrew Kuchins (2010). *Russia After the Global Economic Crisis*, Washington, DC: Columbia University Press.

Batra, T.S. (1979). *The Security Council and Veto.* Delhi: B.V.Gupta Publishers.

Bhola, P. (2001). *Foreign Policies of India,Pakistan and China.* Delhi: RBSA Publishers.

Bilgrami, S. J. (2004). *Dynamics of sanctions in World Affairs.* New Delhi : Atlantic Publishers and Distributors.

Boulden, Jane, Ramesh Chandra Thakur, Thomas George Weiss (2009). *The United Nations and Nuclear Orders.* USA: United Nations University Press.

C.K. Webster. (1933). *The League of Nations in Theory and Practice.* London : George Allen and Unwin Ltd.

Cilliers, J. (2015, April 8). "Does the UN Security Council need Reform?" World Economic Forum.

Davydov, A. (2020). "China - USA -Russia: Geopolitics and Pandemic". Far Eastern Affairs, Issue 2.

Duane, S. (2002). *Global Capital,Political Institutions and Policy Changes in Developed Welfare States*,U.K: Cambridge University Press.

Freiesleben, J. V. (2020, November 20). Reforms in Security Council. Retrieved on March 14, 2021 https://www.globalpolicy.org/images/pdfs/032008reform.pdf.

Genser, Jared, Bruno Stagno Ugarte (2014) *The United Nations Security Council in the Age of Human Rights.* New York: Cambridge University Press.

Ghosh, P. (2020, November 17). "Terrorism, Covid-19 Vaccine, Self-Reliant India: What PM Modi said at 12th Brics summit 2020". *Hindustan Times.*

Goodrich, L.M (1946) "Charter of the United Nations Commentary and Documents" *Boston: World Peace Foundation.*

Gulati, S., Pal, A., and Bansal, A. (2020). "Fuzzy Evaluation of Impact of Lockdown Amid Corona Virus on Delhi's Pollution". Advances in Mathematics: Scientific Journal.

Harsh.V. Pant, H.S. (2020, September 18). "75 years of UN-Need for Reforms" In Rajya Sabha Channel. (V. Dahiya, Interviewer)

Hayes, Subside, Kiho Yi (2015) *Multifaceted Nature, Security and Civil Society in East Asia: Foreign policies and the Korean Peninsula.* UK: Open Book Publishers.

Hening, Ruth (2010). *The League of Nations Makers of the Modern World.* London: Haus Publishing.

Herzog, S. (1999). "Globalization and Povert Allevation in India". Liberal Times.

Indian Express. (2020, September 22). "UN and the New Multilateralism".

J. Padelford, N. (1948). "The Use of the Veto". International Organization.

Joshi, M. (2020, November 10). "Biden's China Policy". The Tribune.

Kapstein, E.B. (2000). *Winners and Losers in Indian Economy.* International Organizations, Vol. 54, No. 2 Spring.

Kelly-Kate. (2012). *International Organization* (Fifth Edition). London: Routledge, Taylor and Francis Group.

Kohli, A. (2006)." Politics of Economic Growth in India 1980-2005 -Part II: The 1990 and Beyond". Economic and Political Weekly.

Korbel, Josef (2015) *Risk in Kashmir*. USA: Princeton University Press.

Lättilä, V. (2019, May 28). "A New Proposal For UN Security Council Reform". Oxford Research Group.

Lewis, P. (1997, March 21)." U.N.Panel Proposes Expanding Security Council to 24 Members". The NewYork Times.

Lord-Mallam, N. (2012). *The Politics of the United Nations Security Council Reform Paperback*, Latvia: LAP Lambert Academic Publishing.

Lowe, Vaughan, Adam Roberts and Jennifer Welsh (2010). *The United Nations Security Council and War: The Evolution of Thought and Practice since 1945*. UK: Oxford University Press.

Luck, E. (2006). *UN Security Council: Practise and Promises*. New Delhi: Publisher Routledge, 2006.

Maaroof, Mohammad Khalid (1990) *United Nations and Afghanistan Emergency*. New Delhi:Commonwealth Publishers.

Mangone, G. J. (1954). *A Short History of International Organisation*. New York:, Mc Graw Hill.

Menon, S. (2020). *India's Foreign Affairs Strategy*,Impact Series 052020-02. Delhi: Brookings Institutions India Centre.

Mohanty, B. (2012). *Foreign Policy of India in the 21st Century*. New Delhi: New Century Publications.

Munshi, S.A. (2009). *The Intelligent Person Guide to Good Governance*. New Delhi: Sage Publications.

Nadin, P. (2014, August 23). "Vision 2020: A Discussion of UN Security Council Reform". Our World.

Nadin, P. (2016). *UN Security Council Reform* (Global Institutions). Singapore: Publisher : Routledge; 1 edition (3 March 2016).

Nafed, A. (2005). "Permanent Membership in United Nations Security Council: India Diplomatic Initiative and Strategies." India Quarterly, Vol.61,Issue 4.

P. Saksena, K. (1993). *Reforming the United Nations The Challenge of Relevance*. California: Sage Publications.

Padmanabhan, G. S. (2004). *The Writing on the Wall :India Checkmates America 2017.* New Delhi: Manas Publications.

Pramit Pal Chaudhary, F. A. (2020, September 18). "75 years of UN- Need for Reforms" Rajya Sabha Channel, (V. Dahiya, Interviewer).

Ramcharit, S. (1998). *United Nations and World Politics.* New Delhi: Kanishka Publishers, Distributors

Rohan Mukherjee, D. M. (2013, July 20). "India and the UN security Council : An Ambiguous Tale". Economic and Political weekly.

Saksena, K.P. (2000). *Reforming the United Nations: The Challenges of Relevance.* London: Sage Publications.

Samarsen (1996). *United Nations and the Global Challenge.* New Delhi: Kanishka Publishers.

Saxena, S. (2020, September 16). "IBSA Calls for Speedy Global Efforts to Reform UN Security Council". Hindustan Times.

Sen, S. (1996). *United Nations and the Global Challenge.* New Delhi: Kanishka Publishers Distributors.

Sharma, Prem Mohan (1978). *Politics of Peace and UN General Assembly* New Delhi: Abhinav Publications.

Shivam, R. K. (2017). *India's Foreign Policy Nehru to Vajpayee.* Delhi: Arjun Publishing House.

Singh, L.P. (1986). *United Nations and the Birth of States.* New Delhi, Gitanjali Publishing House.

Singh, M. (2018). *India's Relation with South Asian Countries.* New Delhi: The Readers Paradise.

Singh, S. K. (2017). *India's Foreign Policy.* New Delhi : Manak Publications.

Sud, Usha (1983). *Decolonization to World Order.* New Delhi: National Publishing House.

Talukdar, S. (2020, May 8). "India's walked a fine Foreign Policy line during COVID-19 Crisis; test ahead lies in how Modi handles Big Powers". First Post.

United Nation (2020) https://www.un.org/securitycouncil/content/functions-and-powers. (n.d.). Retrieved November 10, 2020, from https://www.un.org/ securitycouncil/ content/functions-and-powers.

Webster, C. (1933). *The League of Nations in Theory and Practice.* London: George Allen

Wet, Erika de (2004). *The Chapter VII Powers of the United Nations Security Council.* USA:Hart Publishing.

Worsnip, B. P. (2009, February 19). " UN Launches talk to Expand Security Council".

Zhenqiang, P. (2005). "On Reforms of the UN Security Council". Online Info-Service Vol. 2/2005.

Chapter - 2

UNSC: Organizational Set Up and Functions

The UN Security Council is the core of the global security system and has the legitimate power to take actions to deal with the threats and aggressions among states. The Security Council is the most powerful apex body of United Nations having Headquarter at New York, United States is a pre-eminent authoritative body within UN system (Knight, 2003).

Security Council held its first session on 17 January 1946 at Church House, Westminster, and London. The Security Council adopted its provisional rules of procedure at its first meeting. At the first meeting, the Council appointed a Committee of Experts consisting of representatives of all its eleven members to examine and report on the rules of procedure. In the United Nations Charter Article 23 to Article 32 relates to structure of U.N. Security Council as given in Table No.2.1.

Table 2.1: Chapter V of UN Charter

Composition of Security Council	Article 23
Functions and powers of Security Council	Article 24-26 of the Charter
Voting Procedure in Security Council	Article 27
Procedure of Security Council	Article 28-32 of Charter

Source: https://research.un.org/en/docs/peacekeeping/sc

Size of the Council

The Charter provided that the Security Council should consist of five permanent members and six other members elected by the General Assembly for two-years terms, three members being elected each year. The names of the five permanent members were listed in the Charter did not exist in the case of the League Council. The principle followed in determining the permanent members was that those members of the organization who had made major contribution to the winning of the war and who consequently would be expected to make the major contributions in keeping the peace should be in position to exercise corresponding influence on substantive decisions of the Council and will be given permanent membership (Leland, 1972).

A proposal was introduced at San Francisco to increase the number of non-permanent members on the Council, but the major powers successfully resisted these pressures. The distribution of seats on the Council had long been a source of dissatisfaction, and with the rapid increase in the membership of the United Nations after 1955, pressures mounted for increasing size of Security Council. However, the Soviet Union opposed the move on the ground that the Charter could not be amended so long as China was not represented in the United Nations and no amendment could come into effect without the ratification of all of the permanent members of the Security Council.

The first proposal to increase the size of the Council by amending Article 23 was introduced by a group of Latin American states at 1956 session of the General Assembly. It called for raising the number of non-permanent members from six to eight but could not pass. When the proposal came to a vote in the General Assembly in 1960, it was defeated in large part because of the insistence of a group of Asian and African States that the approval of amendment be linked with a call for an immediate redistribution of Council seats. In 1963, agreement was finally reached to increase the number of elected members from six to ten; this amendment came into force on September 1, 1965 (Res, 1963).The Council is now composed of 15 member's five permanent members and ten non-permanent members.

Composition of Security Council

Composition of Security Council was given in the following Articles of UN Charter.

Article 23

1. The Security Council shall consist of fifteen Members of the United Nations. The Republic of China, France, the Union of Soviet Socialist Republics, the United Kingdom of Great Britain and Northern Ireland, and the United States of America shall be permanent members of the Security Council. The General Assembly shall elect ten other members of the United Nations to be non-permanent members of the Security Council, due regard being specially paid, in the first instance to the contribution of members of the United Nations to the maintenance of international peace and security and, and also to equitable geographical distribution.

2. The non-permanent members of the Security Council shall be elected for a term of two years. In the first election of the non-permanent members after the increase of the membership of the Security Council from eleven to fifteen, two of the four additional members shall be chosen for a term of one year. A retiring member shall not be eligible for immediate re-election.

3. Each member of the Security Council shall have one representative

Permanent Members

The Charter lists the permanent members of the Security Council as the "Republic of China, France, the Union of Soviet Socialist Republics, the United Kingdom of Great Britain and Northern Ireland, and the United States of America." Among the permanent members the People's Republic of China replaced Republic of China in 1971and The Russian Federation succeeded the Soviet Union in 1991.

The concurrence of all five of them is, with few exceptions, needed before the Security Council can make any substantive decision (Article 27).

No amendment to the Charter can become effective unless ratified by all the permanent members (Article 108 and 109).

Indeed, the Charter itself could not come into force until all five had deposited their instruments of ratification (Article 110). The special position of the permanent members with regard to the maintenance of international peace and security is emphasized in other articles. They alone are members of the Military Staff Committee (Article 47). As a "transitional" arrangement (Article 106), these five powers were to "consult" with a "view to joint action on behalf of the Organization" for maintaining peace until the time when the entry into force of arrangements under Article 43 enabled the Security Council to exercise its responsibilities under Article 42 (Rich, 1969).

Ten Non-Permanent Members

Each year General Assembly that consist of 193 members elects five non-permanent members for a two year term (with end of term year) On the basis of regional distribution 10 non-permanent seats are distributed. Five for African and Asian states, one for Eastern Europe States, two for Latin America and Caribbean states, and two for Western Europe and other states. Thus five non-permanent members are elected every year by the General Assembly for a period of two years and five non-permanent members retire each year. The Presidency is held in rotation by each member for a period of one month.

Election of Security Council in 2020

On 17th June in 74th Session of UN General Assembly elections for Security Council were scheduled, since UN Headquarter were closed because of Covid-19 Pandemic in mid-March then according to General Assembly decision adopted on 29th May member states casted ballots during designated time slots at General Assembly Hall. Casting of ballots was covered live on UN webcast and President of General Assembly oversees the process on site.

Five seats available for elections in 2020 were as following

- One seat for the African group (previously held by South Africa)

- One seat for Asia Pacific group (previously held by Indonesia)
- One seat for Latin America and Caribbean Group (previously held by Dominican Republic)
- Two seats for the Western Europe and others Groups (previously held by Belgium and Germany).

Five non-permanent members were Estonia, Niger, St. Vincent, and the Grenadines, Tunisia and Vietnam were elected to the council for tenure of two years beginning from January 2020. St Vincent and the Grenadines was the smallest nation ever who has secured seat in Security Council (PTI, Asia Pacific Group endorses india's candidature for UNSC non permanent seats, 2019). The five new members elected in 2020 who took up their seats on 1 January 2021 and will serve until December 2022 (Security Council Report, 2020). Were India, Norway, Ireland, Mexico and Kenya (PTI, India elected Non permanent member of UN security Council, 2020).

Table 2.2: Composition of Security Council as on 1.1.2021

Permanent Members	Non-Permanent members
U.K	Estonia (till 2021)
France	Niger (till 2021)
United States of America	Saint Vincent and the Grenadines (till 2021)
The Russian Federation	Tunisia (till 2021)
People's republic of China	Vietnam (till 2021)
	India (till 2022)
	Ireland (till 2022)
	Norway (till 2022)
	Mexico (till 2022)
	Kenya (till 2022)

Source: www.un.org

It has been observed that many countries were elected as non-permanent members of Security Council several times as given in following chart.

Graph 2.1: Non-Permanent United Nations Security Council Members Elected with the most terms since 1946

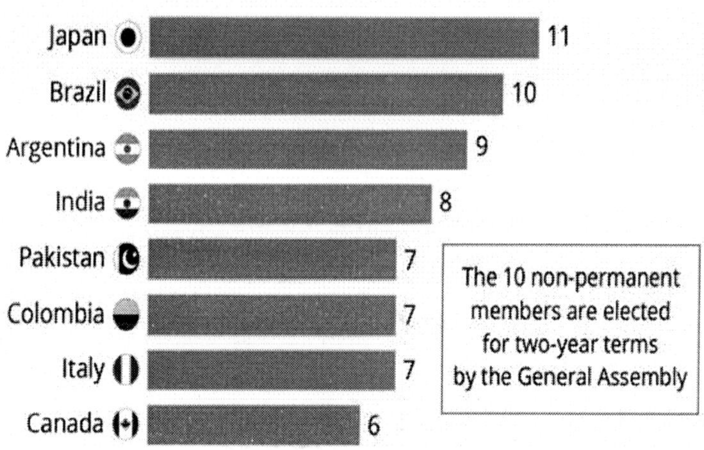

Source: www.un.org

India has served as a non-permanent member of the UNSC for seven terms, viz. in 1950 – 1951, 1967 – 1968, 1972 – 1973, 1977 – 1978, 1984 – 1985, 1991 – 1992, and 2011 – 2012. India was again elected for the term 2021-22.

Functions and Powers of Security Council

Article 24

1. In order to ensure prompt and effective action by the United Nations, its Members confer on the Security Council primary responsibility for the maintenance of international peace and security, and agree that in carrying out its duties under this responsibility the Security Council acts on their behalf.

2. In discharging these duties the Security Council shall act in accordance with the Purposes and Principles of the United

Nations. The specific powers granted to the Security Council for the discharge of these duties are laid down in Chapters VI, VII, VIII, and XII.

3. The Security Council shall submit annual and, when necessary, special reports to the General Assembly for its consideration.

Article 25

The Members of the United Nations agree to accept and carry out the decisions of the Security Council in accordance with the present charter.

Article 26

In order to promote the establishment and maintenance of international peace and security with the least diversion for armaments of the world's human and economic resources, the Security Council shall be responsible for formulating, with the assistance of the Military Staff Committee referred to in Article 47, plans to be submitted to the Members of the United Nations for the establishment of a system for the regulation of armaments (un.org/securitycouncil).

Article 24 establishes the basic principle of the "primary responsibility" of the Security Council for the maintenance of international peace and security. By the term of this article, members not only "confer" this responsibility on the Council but agree that in carrying out its duties the Council "acts on their behalf'. Any decisions of the Security Council taken in discharge of its responsibilities must, therefore, be considered as action taken by the Organization as a whole. All members share in any responsibilities the Council assumes and all are subject to any obligation it imposes. Decisions of the Council apply equally to any obligation in favour and those voting against, as well as to those members which, not being represented on the Council; have no opportunity to vote at all. This point has been of Special concern to some of Non-Permanent council members.

Primary Responsibility of Security Council

The "Primary responsibility" for the maintenance of international peace and security upon the Security Council, the founders of the

Organization recognized that organ as best fitted, by virtue of size and composition, to insure "prompt and effective action". This effort to associate responsibility with power was viewed by many as one of the major advances of the Charter of the United Nations over the League system, in which the powers of the Council and the Assembly were largely identical.

At the San Francisco Conference, numerous attempts were made to diminish the primacy of the Security Council, principally through enlarging the powers and responsibilities of the General Assembly and regional organizations. In both respects, provisions were added to the Charter spelling out these responsibilities in greater detail, but the primary position of the Council, particularly with regard to enforcement measures, remained intact, the text of Article 243 corresponds to the Dumbarton Oaks draft with the single addition of a paragraph requiring the Council to submit reports for the consideration of the Assembly. Article 24 has been most often used in statements to the effect that, if the Council did not act or did not take a particular action, it would be failing to discharge the responsibility conferred upon it under the Charter. Closely related are the frequent statements that it is the Security Council, rather than some other organ or agency, which should act. This point has been raised in connection with actions by regional organizations, subsidiary bodies, the Secretary-General, and most especially the General Assembly.

Thus General Assembly is a forum of discussion, considerations and recommendations. The Security Council has action for its role.

The functions and powers assigned to the Security Council under the charter are the following:

- To maintain international peace and security in accordance with the principles and purposes of the UN;
- To investigate any dispute or situation that might lead to international friction and to recommend methods of adjusting such disputes or the terms of settlement;

- To determine the existence of a threat to the peace or an act of aggression and to recommend what action should be taken;
- To call on members to apply economic sanctions and other measures not involving the use of force in order to prevent or stop aggression;
- To take military action against an aggressor; and
- To formulate plans for the establishment of a system to regulate armaments.

The Security Council also is empowered to exercise the trusteeship functions of the UN in areas designated as "strategic" (only the Trust Territory of the Pacific Islands was so designated). The Council, however, does not consider itself obliged to respect the verdicts of the ICJ. The Security Council takes its decisions on the issues brought before it by member states on the basis of the political equations prevailing on each occasion.

The Council also recommends to the General Assembly the admission of new members and the appointment of the Secretary-General and, together with the General Assembly, elects the judges of the International Court of Justice. (nationsencyclopedia.com)

General Powers

"Specific powers granted to the Security Council" are laid down in chapters VI, VII, VIII and XII of the Charter. The general powers of the Security Council came up the first time the Council was called upon to consider a matter relating to the maintenance of international peace and security. The specific question was whether the council could retain on its agenda the complaint by Iran against the Soviet Union despite a request by Iran that it be removed. The restricted interpretation of the Council's powers, as most fully developed in a memorandum by the Secretary-General, was that the Council could not retain its jurisdiction over the question in the absence of a specific exercise by the Council of its powers under Chapter VI. The majority of the Council members took a much broader view. The representative of Mexico, for example, held that Article 24 "invests the Council with implied power wider in scope than the specific powers" enumerated in paragraph 2 of that article.

The Security Council during the first years of its operations established the general practice of interpreting the authority of the Council in a broad and flexible manner. Although it is generally accepted that the Council, in the discharge of its responsibilities, can exercise powers beyond those specifically listed in Article 24 (2), this does not mean that these powers are considered unlimited.

Limitations on Powers

The Security Council "shall act in accordance with the Purposes and Principles of the Charter". The reference here is to the specific provisions of Article 1 and 2 of the Charter. In San Francisco Conference, various attempts were made to restrict the powers of the Council even further. Norway sought to alter the terms of Article 24 (2) so as to require the Council to act not only in accordance with "the purposes and principles of Charter" but also in accordance with the "provisions of the Charter, and the consideration that no solution should be imposed upon a State of a nature to impair its confidence in its future security or welfare." This proposal was defeated, as were more indirect efforts to limit the powers of the Council, such as the introduction of a definition of aggression, and the proposed alteration of Article 1 (1), which would have made the phrase "in conformity with the principles of justice and international law" apply not only to the functions of pacific settlement but also to any action taken with regard to threats to the peace, breaches of the peace, and acts of aggression. The competence of the Security Council has been challenged; the discussion has centred on the powers of the Council under Chapters VI and VII of the Charter. Occasionally, Article 24 has been invoked in connection with arguments that nowhere in its Charter are the Security Council authorized to take the kind of action under consideration.

Binding Force of Decisions

The United Nations under Article 25 are the direct consequence of the authority conferred on the Security Council under Article 24. If members agree that the Security Council, in discharging its "primary responsibility" for the maintenance of international peace and security, acts on their behalf, it is logical that they should also agree to accept and carry out decisions taken by the Council in discharge of that responsibility. At San Francisco, Belgium sought to limit the obligations of members to those decisions taken by the Security Council in exercise of its powers under Chapter VI, VII and VIII of the Charter. Considered unduly restrictive by some delegates, this proposal failed to obtain the necessary two-thirds majority vote. During the debate in the Security Council on the Statute for the Free Territory of Trieste, the Security General cited the rejection of the Belgian amendment to support the conclusion that members were obligated to accept and carry out decisions of the Council, whether taken in accordance with its general or specific powers. The obligation of members under Article 25 is limited, however, to decisions taken "in accordance with the present Charter".

The Dumbarton Oaks draft of this provision prompted questions at the San Francisco Conference as to whether this phrase was intended to define the manner in which the Security Council was to make decisions. The text was therefore redrafted to make it clear that members were obligated to carry out only those decisions of the Council that was legally mandatory. The Repertory of United Nations Practice points out, Article 25 "contains no precise delimitation of the range of decisions to which it relates," and the Security Council "has no occasion found it necessary to define the scope of the obligation incurred by members of the United Nations under Article 25" (Report of UNSC, 2016).

Voting Procedure in the Security Council

The voting formula in the Security Council which was discussed at Dumbarton Oaks and given in Yalta was inserted into the Charter of the United Nations in San Francisco. Article 27 of the Charter reads:

Article 27

1. Each member of the Security Council shall have one vote.
2. Decisions of the Security Council on procedural matters shall be made by an affirmative vote of nine members.

3. Decisions of the Security Council on all other matters shall be made by an affirmative vote of nine members including the concurring votes of the permanent members; provided that, in decisions under Chapter VI, and under paragraph 3 of Article 52, a party to a dispute shall abstain from voting (Fies, 1957).

4. Each member has one vote. On the basis of affirmative vote of any nine members of Security Council decision is taken by Security Council. On substantive matters like application of sanction or investigation of dispute nine affirmative votes including all five members of Security Council is required. Security Council functions continuously and each member is represented at all times in New York City.

Voting of Non-Council Member States

More than 50 United Nations Member States have never been Members of the Security Council. A State which is a Member of the United Nations but not of the Security Council may participate, without a vote, in its discussions when the Council considers that country's interests are affected. Both members and non-members of the United Nations, if they are parties to a dispute being considered by the Council, may be invited to take part, without a vote, in the Council's discussions; the Council sets the conditions for participation by a non-member State.

Procedure in Security Council

Any dispute can be brought before Security Council. Even those countries who are not members of United Nations can bring their dispute before Security Council. On receiving complaint Security Council explores the possibility of peaceful resolution. International peace keeping force can also be authorized by Security Council to diffuse the situation and further negotiation. If Council feels that due to dispute there is threat to peace, a breach of peace or an act of aggression it may call upon UN members to apply diplomatic or economic sanctions as defined in Article 39 of the UN charter. If above mentioned methods prove inadequate, the UN charter allows the Security Council to take military action against the offending nation. Articles relating to Procedure of Security Council are mentioned in following Articles of UN Charter:

Article 28

1. The Security Council shall be so organized as to be able to function continuously. Each member of the Security Council shall for this purpose be represented at all times at the seat of the Organization.
2. The Security Council shall hold periodic meetings at which each of its members may, if it so desires be represented by a member of the government or by some other specially designated representative.
3. The Security Council may hold meetings at such places other than the seat of the Organization as in its judgment will best facilitate its work.

Article 29

The Security Council may establish such subsidiary organs as it deems necessary for the performance of its functions.

Article 30

The Security Council shall adopt its own rules of procedure, including the method of selecting its President.

Article 31

Any Member of the United Nations which is not a member of the Security Council may participate, without vote, in the discussion of any question brought before the Security Council whenever the latter considers that the interests of that Member are specially affected.

Article 32

Any Member of the United Nations which is not a member of the Security Council or any state which is not a Member of the United Nations, if it is a party to a dispute under consideration by the Security Council, shall be invited to participate, without vote, in the discussion relating to the dispute. The Security Council shall lay down such conditions as it deems just for the participation of a state which is not a Member of the United Nations (un.org).

Who can invoke the Security Council

As per Article 35 (1) any member of UN can bring any dispute or any situation of the nature referred to in Article 34,to the attention of Security council or of the General Assembly.

Article 35 (2) A State which is not a member of the United Nations may bring to the attention of the Security Council or the General Assembly any dispute to which it is a party, if it accepts in advance, for the purpose of dispute, the obligations of the pacific settlement provided in the present charter. Such a non-member shall be invited to participate without vote, in the discussion relating to the dispute.

Article 99 of the Charter confers on the Secretary General a right by which he may bring to the attention of Security Council any matter which in his opinion may threaten the maintenance of international peace and Security.

Representatives of non UN members who are not parties to dispute could be invited to participate under Rule 39, if the council considers them competent to supply information or give other assistance.

Naturally, parties argue about a particular dispute or question and they are listened to, most of the time, by members of the Council. Decisions in the form of resolutions are then worked out in ways which are only slightly less opaque.

Committees of Security Council

Military and Staff Committees, sanction Committees Peace keeping forces committee, International Tribunal Committees and various standing and adhoc committees facilitates the work of Security Council.

Meetings of Security Council

The President of Security Council can call a meeting of the council in various circumstances (Rule 1-3).

The responsibility for convening a meeting of Security Council is on the President. According to Rules ordinary meeting of the Council shall be held at any time deemed necessary by the President, but the interval between the meetings shall not exceed 14 days (Rule 1). Meeting can be called at the request of member of the council (Rule 2). Meeting can also be called if the General Assembly makes recommendations to the council, or refers to it any question relating to maintenance of international peace and security under Article 11(2) of the charter (Rule 3). Meeting can also be called if a dispute or situation is brought to the attention of the Council under Article 35 of the Charter (disputes or situation which might lead to international friction or give rise to disputes) or Article 11(3) of the charter (situation which are likely to endanger international peace Security (Rule 3). In an emergency, the President sometimes convenes a meeting even without consultation using his discretion (Sen, United Nations & the Global Challenge, 1996).

Meeting is called sometimes in official mode or, sometimes called through informal consultations. The differences in the two formats are enormous. An open meeting, non-members of the Council are allowed to speak or make statements. A closed meeting, closed door meetings are also formal meetings like open meetings but they are not open to public. No record is maintained of such meetings Media organizations are not allowed to cover these meetings. Council does not release verbatim records of the statement but only issue a communiqué in these meetings.

Functioning of Security Council

Adopting Resolutions

Security Council adopts resolutions to:

- establish peacekeeping
- determine mandates,
- assign tasks, such as:
- maintain peace and security
- facilitate the political process
- protect civilians
- assist in the disarmament, demobilization and reintegration of former combatants

- support the organization of elections
- protect and promote human rights
- assist in restoring the rule of law
- authorize the deployment of troops, as well as any increase or reduction in troop strength as the situation demands
- Most operations' mandates are reviewed every 6 months or year.

At the risk of only a slight exaggeration, it can be said that the members, especially some western permanent members, seem to be allergic to official meetings and prefer to avoid them as much as possible. For maintenance of international peace and Security, Security Council, passes resolutions, imposes sanctions, send peace keeping mission, does Humanitarian interventions and uses its veto power also (www.un.org).

Resolutions

The period from 1945 to 2014, the Security Council has issued 2,195 resolutions. The data analysis of SC resolutions demonstrates that 78 percent of Security Council resolutions address topics related to a specific geo-political area. Out of 743 resolutions,43 percent concern the African continent; 469 decisions comprising 27 percent concern the Middle East region; 321 resolutions comprising 19 percent, concern Europe while 182 resolutions comprising 11 percent, concern other geographical regions. Taken together, the number of SC decisions addressing issues taking place in Africa and in the Middle East is equal to 1,212 out of 1,715, comprising 70 percent. However, SC practice has not been constant over the decades. In the period of time from the origins to the cold war (1945–1991), the majority of resolutions on geo-political areas address issues taking place in the Middle East while in the post-cold war period (1991–2000) equally address issues taking place in Africa and Europe. Finally, the resolutions of the twenty-first century (2001–2014) are characterized by a sharp focus on issues taking place in Africa and a substantial development of thematic, rather than country-specific, resolutions (Simma, 2002). As of 4 December

2020 the Security Council has passed 2554 resolutions since its inception.

Imposing Sanctions

The Security Council can take action to maintain or restore international peace and security under Chapter VII of the United Nations Charter. Sanctions measures, under Article 41, encompass a broad range of enforcement options that do not involve the use of armed force.

The only sanctions that the General Assembly can wield against an uncooperative member are the suspension of the rights and privileges of membership and expulsion from the organization, but even these sanctions can be invoked only on the recommendation of the Security Council.

Countries those have sanctions placed on them includes Angola, Burundi, Ethiopia and Eritrea, Iran, Iraq, Ivory Coast, Liberia, Libya, Nigeria, North Korea, Rwanda, Sierra Leone, Somalia, Sudan and the Former Yugoslavia. Each of these sanction regimes have been followed by Global Policy Forum (globalpolicy.org).

The UN Security Council has experienced greater cooperation, not coordination among its permanent members and has taken decisions which have enhanced its role in international relations. These decisions have eroded and redefined the concept of sovereignty. Between 1988 and late 1989 Security Council established five peace keepings and observer forces to assist settlement of the Iran- Iraq war, The Afghan Angolan and Namibian crisis and interlinked conflicts within Central America. The Iraqi invasion of Kuwait in August 1990 led the Security Council to adopt a mandate authorizing the use of force by coalition of member's states led by United States. In the Gulf crises the UN became an essential instrument for the Geopolitical interests of its most powerful member. Until 1990, mandatory sanctions had been imposed by Security Council against Iraq in 1990, Yugoslavia in 1991, Libya in 1992, Haiti in 1993, UNITA in Angola in 1993 and Sierra Leone in 1997. Highly circumscribed diplomatic sanctions were also adopted against Sudan in 1996. Thus during the years 1990-1996 the Security Council greatly increased resort to economic sanctions as a means to compel compliance with its decisions.

The Security Council authorized the use of force in Bosnia and Somalia in 1992, in Rwanda in connection with Operation Turquoise in Haiti in 1994, In Zaire in 1996 and in Albania in 1997. In Rwanda there was a blatant display of the absence of political will by the Security Council. The UN presence in Bosnia was out of control of department of peace keeping.

In 2003, for the so called 'Coalition of the willing' invaded Iraq without explicit UN mandate (Oudraat, 2000). In 2014, perhaps unsurprisingly, Syria witnessed the Anglo, French, American and Russian interventions, 11 among others, in its territory. When states themselves and in particular, core UN members seek to use force to settle a crisis, the UN system is shaken, and its legitimacy and legality, contested (Moynihan, 2015).

On 30th March 2018 UNMIL completed its mandate the Council expressed its appreciation for its important contribution throughout more than 14 years of operations in Liberia. On 14th November 2018, the Council decided to lift the arms embargo, travel ban, assets freeze and other targeted sanctions imposed on Eritrea by the Security Council. On 21 December 2018, council authorized Security Council to deploy team in Yemen for monitoring implementation of Stockholm Agreement (unite.un.org). Security Council decided to extend a modified sanctions regime against the Central African Republic through 31st January 2020 and decided operation to review and adjust the arms embargo in measures imposed.

Humanitarian Intervention by Security Council

Humanitarian intervention is an act, which seeks to intervene to stop a Government murdering its own people. Article 2(7) of UN Charter prohibits the UN from intervening in matters which are essentially within the jurisdiction of State. The majority of international lawyers argue that the prohibition on the use of force in Article2 (4) of the UN charter renders forcible humanitarian intervention illegal. The only legitimate exception is the right of self-defence in Article 51 of the UN

Charter on the basis of which it is argued that legal right of unilateral and collective humanitarian intervention in society of states (Bilgrami, 2004).

UN Peace Keeping

The UN Department of Peacekeeping Operations was created in 1992 to support this increased demand for such missions. By and large, the new operations were successful in El Salvador and Mozambique. Although Nobel Prize for peace was given to UN Peace keeping force in 1988 yet several of its missions invited criticism also.

The failures most notably the 1994 Rwandan genocide and the 1995 massacre in Srebrenica and Bosnia and Herzegovina led to a period of retrenchment and self-examination in UN peacekeeping. The UN Peacekeeping commitment to protecting cultural heritage dates back to 2012, when there was extensive destruction in Mali. In this matter, the protection of a country's cultural heritage was included in the mandate of a United Nations mission (Resolution 2100) for the first time in history. In addition to many other advances, Italy signed an agreement with UNESCO in February 2016 to create the world's first emergency task force for culture, made up of civilian experts and the Italian Carabineer. An outstanding mission was the deployment of the UN peace mission UNIFIL together with Blue Shield International in 2019 to protect the UNESCO World Heritage in Lebanon. As of 30 June 2019, there are 100,411 people serving in UN peacekeeping operations (86,145 uniformed, 12,932 civilian, and 1,334 volunteers). European nations contribute nearly 6,000 units. Pakistan, India, and Bangladesh are among the largest individual contributors with around 8,000 units each. African nations contributed nearly half the total, almost 44,000 units.

Security Council and the Use of Veto Power

Veto power is enjoyed by permanent members of UNSC. It has been used by these states as per their national and security interests which make its use discriminatory and unjust.293 times vetoes have been used by Security Council. Resolutions of UNSC are vetoed by permanent members of Security Council. As of July 2020 Russia / USSR has used its veto maximum 116 times while United States has used its veto 82 times, U. K. has used its vetoes 29 times while France and China has used its veto 16 times each. France and United Kingdom have not used veto since 1989.

Graph 2.2: Veto's Power used by P5

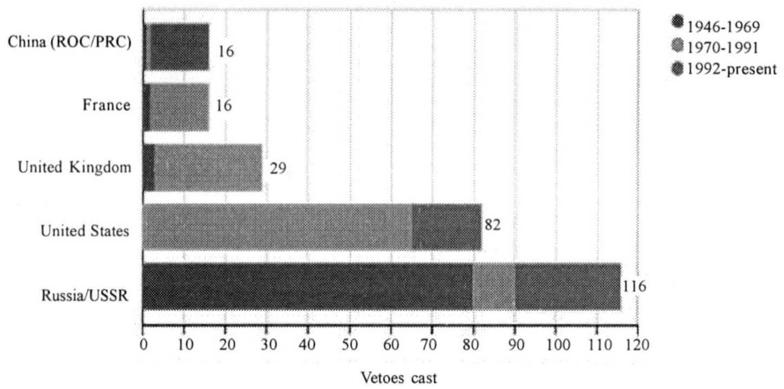

Source: www.un.org

The Security Council politically used veto to protect and advance their individual interests, thus led to irresponsible use of power (Batra, The Security Council & Veto, 1979).

UN Peacekeeping Missions and the Human Rights

Human Rights violations by United Nations soldiers, peacekeepers and employees were reported various times. Human trafficking, and forced prostitution were reported in those areas where peacekeeping missions were undertaken by UN. Reporters witnessed a rapid increase in prostitution in Cambodia and Mozambique after UN peacekeeping forces moved in. In the 1996 UN study "The Impact of Armed Conflict on Children", former first lady of Mozambique Graça Machel documented: "In 6 out of 12 country studies on sexual exploitation of children in situations of armed conflict prepared for the present report, the arrival of peacekeeping troops has been associated with a rapid rise in child prostitution."

Gita Sahgal spoke out in 2004 with regard to the fact that prostitution and sex abuse crops up wherever humanitarian intervention efforts are set up. It was observed during the study that "The issue with the UN is that peacekeeping operations unfortunately seem to be doing the same thing that other militaries do. Even the guardians have to be guarded".

Table 2.3: Confirmed Accounts of Crimes and Human Rights Violations Committed by United Nations Soldiers, Peacekeepers and Employees

A Comparison of Incidents Involving United Nations Peacekeepers, Troops and Employees				
Conflict	United Nations Mission	Sexual abuse	Murder	Extortion/ Theft
Second Congo War	United Nations Mission in the Democratic Republic of Congo	150	3	44
Somali Civil War	United Nations Operation in Somalia II	5	24	5
Sierra Leone Civil War	United Nations Mission in Sierra Leone	50	7	15
Eritrean-Ethiopian War	United Nations Mission in Ethiopia and Eritrea	70	15	0
Burundi Civil War	United Nations Operation in Burundi	80	5	0
Rwanda Civil War	United Nations Observer Mission Uganda-Rwanda	65	15	0
Second Liberian Civil War	United Nations Mission in Liberia	30	4	1
Second Sudanese Civil War	United Nations Mission in Sudan	400	5	0
Côte d'Ivoire Civil War	United Nations Operation in Côte d'Ivoire	500	2	0
2004 Haitian coup d'état	United Nations Stabilization Mission in Haiti	110	57	0
Kosovo War	United Nations Interim Administration Mission in Kosovo	800	70	100
Israeli–Lebanese conflict	United Nations Interim Force in Lebanon	0	6	0

Source: https://digitallibrary.un.org/

Failure of Security Council during Pandemic Covid-19

In September 2014 Security Council adopted a resolution declaring Ebola a threat to international peace and security and urged the world to send more health workers and assistance to hard hit countries of

Liberia, Sierra Leone and Guinea but during Covid-19 pandemic Security Council paralyzed. Paralysis came at a time when United States was pressing 15 nation council to adopt a resolution for blaming China for spread of Corona virus (Lynch, 2020). The silence of UNSC under China's Presidency in March 2020 on issue of human security reflected that it is not fit for handling the challenges (Hindu, 2020). There is need for reforming and restructuring UNSC to strengthen and equip UN system to meet contemporary and future challenges (Mehrish, 2007).

Summary

Security Council maintains international peace and security, investigate disputes, methods of adjusting disputes, formulates plan for regulation of armaments, determine existence of threats, apply economic sanctions, takes military action against aggressor, recommend admission of new members, exercise trusteeship functions of United Nations in strategic areas and recommend to the General Assembly the appointment of the Secretary General and together with General Assembly elect the judges of the International Court of Justice. As of 4 December 2020 UNSC has passed 2554 resolutions. 293 times vetoes have been used by Security Council. Resolutions of UNSC are also vetoed by permanent members of Security Council. During Covid-19 pandemic Security Council paralyzed. There is need for reforming and restructuring UNSC to strengthen and equip UN system to meet contemporary and future challenges.

References

Abbi, R. (2017). *United Nations Organization: Its role in Third World Countries.* New Delhi: The Readers Paradise.

Bussemaker, N. (2020, September 16). *https://www.cfr.org/backgrounder/un-security-council.* Retrieved november 19, 2020, from UN Security council.

Fies, H. (1957). *Churchill Roosevelt Stalin: The War they Waged and the Peace.* New Jersey.

Freiesleben, J. V. (2020, November 20). *Reforms in Security Council.* Retrieved from https://www.globalpolicy.org/images/pdfs/032008reform.pdf.

General, R. O. (2005). *"In Larger Freedom: Towards Development, Security and Human Rights for all".* http://www.globalpolicy.org/images/pdfs/followupreport.pdf.

Geneva., I. C. (1940). International Consultative group of Geneva. *'Causes of the Peace Failure'1919-1939,* 363.

Ghosh, P. (2020, November 17). "Terrorism, Covid-19 Vaccine, Self-Reliant India: What PM Modi said at 12th BRICS Summit 2020". *Hindustan Times.*

Harsh.V.Pant, H. S. (2020, September 18). "75 years of UN-Need for Reforms" In Rajya Sabha Channel. (V. Dahiya, Interviewer)

https://www.cfr.org/backgrounder/un-security-council.

Indian Express. (2020, September 22). "UN and the New Multilateralism ".

J. Padelford, N. (1948). "The Use of the Veto". *International organization.*

Kelly-Kate. (2012). *International Organization (*Fifth Edition*).* London: Routledge,Taylor and Francis Group.

Knight, W. A. (2003). *The Future of the UN Security Council :Questions of Legitimacy and Representation in Multilateral Governance.* In R. T. Andrew F. Cooper.John English, *Enhancing Global Governance* (pp. 19-37). Delhi: Bookwell.

Lättilä, V. (2019, May 28). "A New Proposal For UN Security Council Reform". *Oxford Research Group.*

Lavanya, R. (1995). *"Democratization of the United Nations". Economic and Political Weekly,.* New York.

Leland, M. G. (1972). *"The United Nations ".* New York: The Free Press.

Lewis, P. (1997, March 21)." U.N.Panel Proposes Expanding Security Council to 24 Members". *The NewYork Times.*

Lynch, C. (2020, March 27). "UN Security Council Paralyzed as Contagion Rages". *Foreign policy Magazine.*

Mehrish, B. (2007). *The United Nations in the New Millennium : A changing scenerio.* Delhi: Academic excellence.

Mehrish, B. N. (2007). *The United Nations in the New millennium : A Changing scenerio.* India: Academic excellence.

Mingst, M. P. (2010). *International Organizations,The Politics and processes of Global Governance.* New Delhi: Viva Books.

Moynihan, H. (2015). "Assessing the Legal Basis for UK Military Action in Syria".

Nadin, P. (2014, August 23). "Vision 2020: A Discussion of UN Security Council Reform". *Our World.*

Natalino, P. N. (2013). "The European Union and the Reform of the UN Security Council:Toward a new regionalism?".

Nations, U. *Charter chapter 18, article 109, par 3.* New York. Retrieved from United Nations: http://www.un.org/en/documents/charter/chapter18.shtml.

Nations, U. *https://www.un.org/securitycouncil/content/functions-and powers.* Retrieved December 12, 2020, from United Nations: https://www.un.org/securitycouncil/content/functions-and-powers

Oudraat, C. D. (2000). 'Intervention in Internal Conicts: Legal and Political Conundrums'. *Carnegie Endowment for International Peace. Global Policy Program.*

P.Saksena, K. (1993). *Reforming the United Nations The Challenge of Relevance.* California: Sage Publications.

Pease, K.K. S. (2012). *International Organizations.* London: Routledge.

Pramit Pal Chaudhary, F. A. (2020, September 18). "75 years of UN- Need for Reforms"Rajya Sabha Channel. (V. Dahiya, Interviewer)

PTI. (2019, June 26)." Asia Pacific Group Endorses India's Candidature for UNSC Non Permanent Seats". *Business Lines.*

PTI. (2020, June 18). "India elected Non permanent member of UN Security Council". *The Print.*

Report, C.D.M. (2016). "Non-Consenus Decision-Making in the Security Council: an Abridged History' Security Council Report".

Res, G. (1963). "The United Nations". New York.

Retrieved April,2020 from https://www.globalpolicy.org/security-council/index-of-countries-on-the-security-council-agenda/sanctions.html.

Retrieved December, 2019 from unite.un.org.

Retrieved December, 2020 from https://www.nationsencyclopedia.com/United-Nations/The-Security-Council-functions and powers.html.

Retrieved January, 2020 from www.un.org.

Retrieved March, 2020 from www.indiatoday.in.

Rich, L. M. (1969). *Charter ofthe United Nations.* New York: Colcombia University Press.

Roche, E. (2020, September 23). "India,three other Nations call for UN Security Council Revamp". *mint.e paper.*

S.J.R. Bilgrami. (2004). *Dynamics of Sanctions in World Affairs.* New Delhi: Atlantic Publishers and Distributors.

Saxena, S. (2020, September 16). "IBSA Calls for Speedy Global Efforts to Reform UN Security Council". *Hindustan Times.*

SecurityCouncil(2020). "Security Council Report".

Sen, S. (1996). *United Nations and the Global Challenge.* New Delhi: Kanishka Publishers Distributors.

Simma, B. S.P. (2002). "Article 27—Voting. In The Charter of the United Nations: A Commentary". *The Charter of the United Nations: A Commentary.*

Stephen, S. (1997). "Can the United Nations Reform?" *World Policy Journal.*

The Hindu (2020, March27).UN Security council yet to discuss coronavirus crisis under China's Presidency.

United Nations (2020). https://www.un.org/en/sections/un-charter/chapter-v/index.html. Retrieved 12 11, 2020, from United Nations: https://www.un.org/en/sections/un-charter/chapter-v/index.html.

Worsnip, B. P. (2009, February 19). Reuter. "UN Launches Talk to Expand Security Council".

Zhenqiang, P. (2005). "On Reforms of the UN Security Council". *Online Info-Service Vol. 2/2005.*

Chapter - 3

Reforms in Security Council

One of the central aspects of the reforms and restructuring the UN system is the democratization and enlargement of Security Council. Reforms and reorganization of Security Council has been more or less a continuous process from the very inception of the Security Council (Saksena, 1993). The Security Council is the most powerful organ of the United Nations. The decisions of the council are known as United Nations Security Council resolutions (Abbi, 2017). The Charter has given it primary responsibility for the maintenance of global peace and security and its decisions are binding for all Member States. Its limited geographical balance combined with five exclusive permanent seats that have veto powers, however, makes the Security Council less representative than desired by many member states especially emerging 'middle' powers and they are increasingly calling for a restructuring of the Council. A few permanent members use it as an instrument for justifying or imposing their policies and preferences which is contrary to the spirit of UN Charter thus need of democratisation and enlargement of the Security Council is felt (Mehrish B. , 2007).Reform efforts are important because they will make Security Council more credible as an inclusive Global institution (Kelly-Kate, 2012). Reforms in Security Council are required on following grounds.

Multilateralism in the World Order

It is no longer bipolar situation of the world order now Multilateralism is big question today as in the present phase of multilateralism larger countries asking for fair share. Japan and

Germany have also emerged as economic power while India has also emerged as economic as well as political power. These emerging nations also wants to play dominant role and enjoy equal status with P5. Human Rights and democracy are important issues in world order and are not effectively dealt by United Nations (Harsh.V.Pant, 2020).

Future of multilateralism that the world order is facing both from existing power structure and emerging power structure is putting the UN structure under strain. American first policy on one hand and refusal of China to abide by multilateralism set another challenge. Multilateralism at cross roads failed during Pandemic Covid-19 and the biggest challenge before it to establish harmony between existing structure and emerging structures (Pramit Pal Chaudhary, 2020).

UNSC and the Stagnated Membership

The membership of the Security Council has changed very little since its inception in 1945, even though the number of UN member states has almost quadrupled since then and the relative power of member states has changed significantly. Addition of four non-permanent seats in 1965 was the only change in membership made. African states call the under-representation of Africa as historical injustice.

Failure of the Security Council

Many critics charge that the council's structure does not reflect current geopolitical realities. The council was expanded from six elected members to ten in 1965 and in 1971.The People's Republic of China took the permanent seat previously occupied by the Republic of China (Taiwan). Since then the body composition of UNSC has remained the same. Regional powers such as Brazil, Germany, India, Japan, Nigeria, and South Africa have sought to enlarge the council or secure permanent seats. Others have called for France to cede its permanent seat to the European Union in the wake of Brexit, especially after France and Germany decided to share the presidency of the council for two months in 2019. The debate about expansion is often framed as a trade-off between legitimacy and efficacy. Saudi Arabia took the unprecedented step of declining a Security Council seat in October 2013, announcing that it would not serve in the further absence of institutional reform. While R2P criticize the Security Council and its members for a lack of political will.

Unequal Security Council

The differences between permanent and non-permanent seats produce a highly unequal and inefficient Security Council. The five permanent members (P5) – Britain, France, United States, Russia and China possess permanent seats and have the privilege of the veto on the other hand the status of non-permanent members is low.

Abuse of Veto Power by P5

No feature of United Nations activity has raised more doubts about the ability of International Organizations to assure peace and security than the frequent use of veto power by Security Council (Padelford, 1948).On many occasions, the P5 have abused their veto powers. In total 263 vetoes have been exercised since 1946, the year after the UN charter was officially ratified

Table 3.1: Veto Power used by P5 (till July 2020)

Name of P5	No. of times Veto used
Russia	116
U.S.A.	82
U.K.	29
France	16
China	16

Source: https://research.un.org/en/docs/peacekeeping/sc

It is evident from analysis of above table that Veto power has been used maximum by U.S.S.R.As of July 2020,Russia has used its veto 116 times, United States 81 times, UK 29 times, France 16 times and China 16 times. France and United Kingdom have not used their veto power since 1989. Moving the activities of the Security Council behind closed doors where threats of veto are made in private kills the democratic spirit of Security Council.

Poor Performance of UNSC in Maintaining International Peace and Security

Performance of the Security Council in maintaining international peace and security has been poor. In Somalia, Bosnia and Rwanda it failed in its actions. In Somalia, the strategy was counterproductive and Washington's time table for the mission too arbitrary. In Bosnia, the operation was undermanned and the Security Council could not perform effectively to provide adequate protection for the UN safe areas, resulting in the Srebrenica massacre. In Rwanda Security Council refusal to strengthen the peacekeeping force once the genocide began doomed the operation. Britain, the United States and France all avoided using the term "genocide" to escape their responsibility to intervene. France actually supported the Rwandan government and provided it with arms and ammunition even during the genocide. Moreover interventions in Iraq (2003) and Kosovo (1999) proceeded without Security Council approval. Security Council also failed to act to resolve crisis in Crimea, Syria and Yemen.

United Nations' Conflict-Management Capacity

Peacekeeping crises of 1990s in Somalia, the former Yugoslavia, and Rwanda were criticised. The United Nations also suffered humiliating defeats in the Balkans, where peacekeepers were used as human shields in the siege of Sarajevo and failed to protect civilians in the designated safe area of Srebrenica from massacre. In 2016, an investigation revealed a series of sexual assaults in the Central African Republic, where at least twenty-five minors were abused by forty-one peacekeeping soldiers from Burundi and Gabon. Peacekeepers deployed in Haiti have faced intense criticism for widespread sexual exploitation, as well as for sparking a cholera outbreak that has killed thousands since 2010.Therefore sexual exploitation is another criticism often citied (Bussemaker, 2020).

Ineffectiveness of Security Council during Covid-19 Pandemic

The UN has been unable to respond effectively to the once in a century global crisis triggered by the Covid-19. At the UN Security

Council, China blocked serious discussion on the origin and sources of the crisis. While the US walked out of the World Health Organisation on allegation of supporting China. As a result of its shortcomings, reform of the Security Council has been deemed necessary (Indian Express, 2020).

Following efforts have been done the direction of Security Council Reforms.

Issues before Structural Reforms of the Security Council

First issue is to increase the number of members for geographical representation and enhanced legitimacy, while maintaining a small enough size to ensure efficiency. The Second issue is whether or not to continue the distinction between permanent and non-permanent members. Closely related is the question of whether new permanent members will have veto power. There has been a demand to increase openness and efficiency of the council's work.

The Debate over UNSC Reforms revolves around the following issues:

1. **Representation**

- Council needs greater representation of Africa, Asia, and Latin America.
- Permanent members should better reflect geopolitics and economics.
- Proposed additions : Germany and Japan
- One member each from Africa, Asia, and Latin America, but who and how to select?
- No permanent members
- No new permanent members

2. **Veto Powers**

- Eliminate entirely

- Reduce scope for its use in Chapter VII decisions
- Keep current P-5, but not give new permanent member veto power
- Give all permanent members veto powers

3. Openness

- More open council meeting
- More information on when council meets, nature of discussions, draft resolutions, presidential statements, actions
- More consultations with interested states and NGOs

4. Efficiency

- Size should be large enough to allow greater representation, but small enough to preserve the ability to act.
- Proposed size: 20-24 members.

5. Requirement for Reforms in Security Council

Reforms in Security Council can be possible only through an amendment of Chapter 18 of UN Charter. (www.indiatoday.in, 2020) Charter amendment requires vote of two thirds of general Assembly members and must be ratified by two third members of the UN including all permanent members of the Security Council(Chapter XVIII, Article 108) (Mingst, 2010).Various reforms proposal have been put forth for reforming Security Council as discussed below.

Security Council Reform Proposals from 1945 till 2020

In practice, the only reform of the UNSC that has taken place was in 1963, when the number of non-permanent members was merely increased from six to ten (Natalino, 2013).A more comprehensive reform debate started only in 1991 with the Accra Declaration. This was adopted by the 103 nation-strong, non-aligned groups, sparking a movement and various reactions during the 1990s (Lavanya, 1995).Various scholars have suggested that the veto power is vital in the interest of the permanent members and that its removal or extension could undermine their participation in the UN or the survival of the UN itself (Stephen S. , 1997).

The permanent members of the UNSC, which formed the core of the allied states, were to keep peace and if necessary, to apply the use of force to do so. It was expected that these nations would contribute largely to troop contingents for such missions. Partly because of that, the permanent members demanded veto rights for UNSC decisions, as well as a high majority threshold for the adoption of resolutions, in order not to become outvoted by smaller UN member states. Currently, some rising powers may be in a similar position to that which the smaller UN members earlier occupied. Compared to the situation prevailing in 1945 however, today there are rising powers that seek a greater role in shaping global governance institutions, but the relationship between military, economic and political weight is weaker, and therefore it is less evident which actors should be members of the UNSC.

The argument currently prevails that the present UNSC set-up no longer reflects the current global power distribution. In particular rising powers, such as Brazil, India and South Africa, but also others such as Nigeria, have voiced their demands for greater representation in the UNSC. Discussion also centres on the number of potential new permanent seats to be established, compared to non-permanent ones and whether new permanent seats should also imply veto power. Since the creation of the UN there have been several reform efforts, including proposals on a reform of the formal composition of the UNSC.

The Security Council held its first session on 17 January 1946 at the Church House in London. Present were the five permanent members: China, France, the Soviet Union, the United Kingdom, and the United States as well as six non-permanent members chosen on a regional, two-year basis. While there is general agreement that the Security Council needs to be reformed, there is extensive disagreement on exactly how, making the issue both extremely divisive and contentious.

Germany and Japan: The UNSC Permanent Seats Contenders

Germany and Japan both began advocating for permanent seats for themselves. The two countries had contributed heavily to the Gulf War efforts, and dramatically increased their contributions to the United Nations as a whole. Simultaneously, public opinion in the two countries began to favour an increased involvement in world affairs. By 1992, Japan and Germany had become, respectively, the second and third largest contributors to the regular budget of the UN. Like Germany and Japan, Italy too had moved well beyond its 1945 status, and by 1992 ranked almost as high a contributor to both the UN regular budget and to its peacekeeping operations. Initially, Italy clearly considered their country a serious contender for a possible permanent seat. However, with the development of the European Union and the prospects of an eventual common EU foreign policy, the Italians instead opted to intensify their resistance against a permanent seat for Germany and work for increased European integration. It soon became apparent that talks on Security Council reform had the instant ability to make regional rivalries flare up. Nigeria, Brazil, South Africa, Egypt, Japan, Germany and India saw the increasing relevance of the Council caused a spark of interest among the membership of the Organization. Suddenly the Security Council was engaged in conflicts around the world.

Uniting for Consensus (Coffee-Club)

Uniting for consensus is a movement nicknamed the Coffee Club, started under the leadership of Italy that developed in 1990 in opposition to the possible expansion of the permanent seats in the United Nations Security council.

Table 3.2: Coffee Club Members

Country	Continent	UN Budget (in percentage)	Member of the UN Since
Argentina	South America	0.892	1945
Canada	North America	2.721	1945
Italy	Europe	3.748	1955
Malta	Europe	0.016	1964
Mexico	North America	1.435	1945
Pakistan	Asia	0.093	1947
South Korea	Asia	2.23	1991
Spain	Europe	2.033	1955
Turkey	Europe	1.018	1945

Source: www.un.org

Italy, Spain, Argentina, Canada, Mexico, Malta, Turkey, South Korea and Pakistan as well as some other countries called for the creation of more non-permanent seats with members to be elected on a regional basis, while fiercely resisting adding any new permanent seats According to Coffee Club permanent seats would violate the principle of sovereign equality and create new center of power, both within and outside the United Nations.

Uniting for Consensus (UFC)

On 16 February 2005, the Coffee Club (Argentina, Colombia, Mexico, Kenya, Algeria, Italy, Spain, Pakistan and South Korea) adopted a document entitled Uniting for Consensus, which subsequently became the name of the group. The document was originally drafted by Italy, and the new name was meant to convey that the group favoured a broad negotiated solution. Uniting for Consensus (UFC) consists of various states including Italy, Spain, Argentina, Canada, Mexico, South Korea and Pakistan which oppose the G4 and the addition of any new permanent seats. The UFC would instead add only non-permanent seats and preferably abolish the veto or at least restrict its use. Uniting for Consensus group maintained a firm stand on this issue, and they were later joined by Qatar, Turkey, Ghana, Costa Rica, Ghana, Costa Rica, Canada, Morocco, San Marino, United Arab Emirates, Bangladesh, and the representative of the Arab League.

Razali Proposal

In 1997 a proposal to enlarge United Nations Security Council from its present 15 members to 24 was proposed by Razali Ismail of Malaysia who was president of General Assembly. Of the nine new seats five would be permanent members and four would rotate in two years. New members will not be given veto power. Plan calls for election of two permanent council members from the industrial world. The other three permanent members would be drawn from Africa, Asia and Latin America respectively. Italy opposed it for enlarging Security Council support of two third of general Assembly and ratification by national legislatures of two third of all members was required (Lewis, 1997).

Kofi Annan's Proposal

In December 2004, Secretary General Kofi Annan proposed changes to Security Council. Reform plan included structural and cultural reforms. Structural reforms were regarding expansion in membership of council from 15 to 24 while changes in working practices were related to broaden its scope of mission. According to that report, one alternative would add six new permanent members as well as three new two-year term members. The other would create a new tier of 8 semi-permanent members chosen for immediately renewable four-year terms and one additional two-year term seat to the existing 10.

There was already tough competition for those permanent seats by a group of countries. Candidates include Brazil, Germany, India, Japan, Egypt and either Nigeria or South Africa was likely candidates. Each of them claims to have good reasons for the seat, but almost all of them face strong opposition by some, if not all, their neighbouring countries. Under the circumstances, the expansion of the UNSC would be stalled if there is no better understanding what the correct criteria should be for the selection of possible permanent members of the UNSC, who are truly able to contribute to the better performance of the future UNSC. Both the panel's report and Annan mention four principles to that end:

(1) They should, in honouring Article 23 of the Charter, increase the involvement in decision-making of those who contribute maximum to the United Nations financially, militarily and diplomatically, specifically in terms of contributions to United Nations assessed budgets, participation in mandated peace operations, contributions to voluntary activities of the United Nations in the areas of security and development, and diplomatic activities in support of United Nations objectives and mandates.

(2) They should bring into the decision-making process countries more representative of the broader membership, especially of the developing world;

(3) They should not impair the effectiveness of the Security Council;

(4) They should increase the democratic and accountable nature of the body.

Both Annan's suggestion and the high level panel's report strongly endorse retaining the veto power by the original permanent members of UNSC, and not extending to the new permanent members in the future. This is perhaps a most sensible suggestion. Critics argue that the practice of giving privileged status to these five states makes the Council both undemocratic and often ineffective (Zhenqiang, 2005).

A More Secure World: Our Shared Responsibility (A/59/565)

In December 2004, the Panel released their report it included 101 recommendations for change and a 'grand bargain' for reform of the Security Council. It proposed two models A and B for enlargement, both of which suggested expanding the Council to 24 members. Model A proposed adding six new permanent seats, but with no veto power, and three new two-year term elected seats. Model B created a new category of eight seats, renewable every four years, and one new two-year non-renewable seats. Apparently the panel would have preferred not to include the addition of permanent members, but according to one ambassador, the Secretary-General "strong-armed" the panel into including that option out of fear of alienating Germany and Japan in the upcoming summit.

Group of Four or G4

Germany, Japan, India and Brazil (known later as the Group of Four or G4) formed in 2005 is political cooperative alliance and support each other bid for permanent membership of Security Council.

Map 3.A: Map of G4 Countries

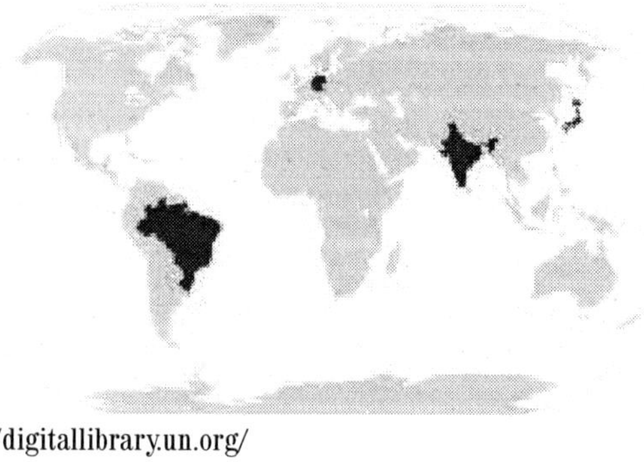

Source: https://digitallibrary.un.org/

Germany and Japan based their claims on the grounds that they are major donors. India did so as the world's second largest country in terms of population, with one of the world's largest economies and the third largest contributor of troops to UN peace-keeping missions. Brazil based its case on being the largest country in terms of territory, population and economy in South America. The two later countries have also increasingly based their claims on their status as leading countries of the 'global south.' G 4 suggested that two African nations should also be included in Security Council while African Union was unable to agree on two nominees: Egypt, Nigeria and South Africa all want claim for UNSC Seat. In September 2019 in 74th Session of United Nations General Assembly reiterated their strong commitment for permanent membership in Security Council.

Small Five or S5

A group of five smaller countries, Switzerland, Singapore, Jordan, Costa Rica and Liechtenstein, had earlier formed a group known colloquially as the Small Five (S5), and they decided to circulate a non-paper and a few drafts on the issue following the summit. In March 2006, they submitted a draft resolution (A/60/L.49) under the agenda item Follow up to the Millennium Summit aimed at achieving a more accountable and transparent Security Council. The draft asked the Council to consult with all Member States on resolutions, and requested that the five permanent members explain every veto to the General Assembly.

Panama Innovative Proposal

In 2007 Panama presented an innovative proposal that allowed for renewable membership but with modification that any member elected to United Nations Security Council for four consecutive terms would acquire PNVM status. Initially, the size of the Council would be increased by adding six non-permanent seats. The new members would be given five-year terms, with the right to immediate re-election. Those are elected four consecutive times would automatically receive permanent seats, but without the right of veto. In the end, no action was taken on this unique "transitional proposal."

Claim of African Group

The African group consists of 54 members of the African Union and is thus the largest regional group by number of member states. The African group, focussed on the need for the international community to correct historical injustice done to Africa by not giving it permanent seat in UNSC. It seeks two permanent and five non-permanent seats for Africa. The African group would preferably abolish the veto, but it insists that as long as the veto exists all permanent members should possess it.

Claim of Arab League

The stated purposes of Arab League are to strengthen ties among member states, coordinate their policies and promote their common interests. The League was founded in Cairo in 1945 by Egypt, Iraq, Jordan and Yemen. The League of Arab group consists of 22 states. The four observers of Arab League are Brazil, Eritrea, India and Venezuela. Arab league demands a permanent Arab seat. It heavily criticises the veto, but does not present any solution to it. Improving partnership with regional organisations is necessary for UNSC. The Arab –Israeli conflict and geopolitical competition in the region, demonstrated by the frequent vetoes cast by US and Russia on Israel-Palestine and Syria respectively has complicated the ability of two bodies to work together. Differences among Arab Leagues countries have been an obstacle to coherent policy positions.

L 69

The L69 consists of some 40 developing countries from all over the world, including Brazil and India.L69 group is a group of developing countries from Africa, Latin America and the Caribbean, Asia and the Pacific. This common bloc has 42 countries and is making efforts for reforms in Security Council. The group is bound by conviction that both permanent and non-permanent categories of membership are imperative to reflect world reality. The group derives its names from the draft document number L 69 that the group had tabled in 2006-2007 It seeks six new permanent seats and six new non-permanent seats balanced across UN regions. Its stance on the veto is similar to that of the African group; either the veto is abolished or extended to all permanent members (Freiesleben, 2020).

Regarding size, proposals range from 25 (G4, UFC) and 26 seats (AU) to 27 (L69). On the issue of categories of membership, however, there is a clear divide between the G4, L69 and AU models on the one hand, and the UFC model on the other. The former support expansion of the UNSC in both permanent and non-permanent categories, whereas the latter insists on expansion only in the non-permanent category, with the new UFC proposal outlining the possibility of longer-term seats allocated to regional groups. Regarding the regional distribution of newly created seats all proposals distribute the additional seats between the established regional blocks within the UNGA, with a small exception made by the L69 and the revised UFC proposals. These two additionally suggested the creation of seats for small island states (L69) or small and middle-sized developing countries, chosen by respective regional groups (UFC).The G4 and UFC propose the same regional distribution (although they differ on the categories of seats), while the AU and L69 proposals both add one more (non-permanent) seat for African states and additionally, the L69 proposes one additional seat for small island states.

Concerning the veto question, G4 and UFC proposals do not seek to touch on the veto privilege to accommodate for P-5 resistance on this issue, whereas the AU as well as the L69 still insists on a veto for new permanent members. Recently, South Africa has started to advocate for compromise strategies. However, the negotiations still appear to be at an impasse.

India, Brazil and South Africa (IBSA)

In September 2019 IBSA gave Joint ministerial statement that failure to reform Security Council has serious implications for international peace and security. The group consisting of India, Brazil and South Africa is usually referred to as IBSA, and has been meeting regularly since the 1990s on development issues; however, this was the first time its name was mentioned in connection with the reform of the Security Council (Saxena, 2020).

The Two-Layered Regional Model for Reforms

As an improvement over the current proposals, Two-Layered Regional Model seeks to eliminate the four identified flaws. First, the Security Council is open to all member states, effectively eliminating exclusivity, regional representation and rotating seats. Second, all privileges including the veto are abolished which makes all member states equal. Third, the current United Nations Regional Groups are modified: the Eastern European Group is abolished and its members integrated to neighbouring groups; a new Middle Eastern and North African group is created; and a new group for Small Island Developing States is created. The goal is to have large regions with socio-cultural links and similar security issues. States that share strong links to two regions can have overlapping memberships in two regional groups. For example, the North African states are strongly linked in their culture, heritage and security issues to the Middle East, but are also strongly tied to Africa by geography and by a long history of membership in the African Union and its predecessor the Organisation of African Unity. As a result, they would most likely prefer to be members in both regional groups. Overlapping membership can also be utilised in other regions such as the Caucasus and Central Asia.

Special arrangements can be considered as well. For example, states located in hostile regional environments in particular, Israel could be granted a standalone status so that they couldn't be dominated by their regional groups. In addition, the P5 could be offered immunity from Security Council resolutions for a period of a few decades to make them more amenable towards reform.

The idea is to use the regional groups in a two-layered voting process where the region in concern and the rest of the world take separate votes on draft resolutions. So, for example, if a draft resolution targeted Zimbabwe, first the African Group would take a vote among its members because Zimbabwe is part of that regional group and then the rest of the UN member states take a separate vote. If both votes gain 60percent support, the draft resolution is adopted. If either vote fails to gain 60 percent support, the draft resolution is abandoned. This formula is followed when the draft resolution concerns intrastate conflict. In cases of interstate conflict there is only a single vote by the Council as a whole.

The design has several benefits. One is that it takes into account the controversial nature of interventions by making it more difficult to intervene in intrastate conflict compared to interstate conflict. Another benefit is that Security Council resolutions gain legitimacy, because all member states have the option to participate in the process. Regions such as Africa and the Middle East have more control over their fates and as such might react faster to emerging crises. As the design emphasises regional responsibility, it decreases the burden of the current permanent members whilst allowing them to intervene more legitimately when there are legitimate threats to international security.

Different Positions of P5 on UNSC Reforms

The P5 are generally hesitant towards reform. Of the five, France and Britain are most open to reform. Whilst all permanent members accept reforms in principle, they have often fought popular reform proposals. For example, when in 2005 it seemed that the G4 and the African group might reconcile their differences; China and Russia declared any reform to be out of question and with the aid of the United States started publicly gathering support to defeat the reform attempt. Similarly, in 2012 intense pressure from the permanent members forced a draft resolution on improving the working methods of the Council to be abandoned.

The P-5 have differing positions, although they share an interest in maintaining the efficiency of the UNSC by favouring if at all only a modest enlargement as well as no expansion of the veto prerogative to new permanent members. France and the United Kingdom are supportive of the G4 and AU proposals, or intermediary compromise models. France even suggested restricting the use of veto in cases of mass atrocities (Lehmann, 2013).

China's Position

China has expressed its support for increased African representation, but at the same time it is negative about Japan and India becoming permanent members, and partly sides with the UFC group.

Russian Position

Russia has stated that it would favour a modest expansion to about 20 or 21 states, possibly including G4 members, but insists on no change to the veto (Nikitin, 2012).

The US Position

Similarly, the United States advocates for a modest increase, and has voiced cautious support for expansion in the permanent category through admitting possibly Japan, India and Brazil, as well as a marginal expansion of the non-permanent member category (Swart, 2013).

Initiatives taken for Reforms

Following initiatives were taken for reforms in Security Council.

UN Peace building Commission

UN Peace building Commission was created in 2006 to strengthen the institution's capacity and to help countries transition through reconstruction and rebuilding from war to peace.

Engendering Peace Keeping

Initiatives were taken for engendering peace keeping missions. Zero Tolerance Policy of UN involves zero sexual contact between peacekeepers and civil population. Zero Tolerance Policy has been complimented by UN efforts to "engender" peacekeeping recommended that Secretary general finds way to integrate women into peacekeeping operations. This resolution brought women's ideas and skills to peacekeeping Table. When women were integrated into peacekeeping mission in Namibia then there were very few cases of sexual harassment and exploitation. Inclusion of women in peacekeeping and advisors in various capacities helped UN to tackle problem of sexual abuse effectively to large extent (Pease, 2012).

Promotion of Discussions in UNSC

Prior to making decisions council members consult with countries contributing troops and materials to peacekeeping operations. SC has invited NGO's representatives to participate in some discussions. In 2000, the council decided to make draft resolutions and presidential statements available to non-members also before their introduction to facilitate inputs from them. Security Council has also increased the number of formal public meetings. To involve those states which are not members "Friends of the Secretary General" have been created.

Principle of Responsibility to Protect (R2P)

In World Summit 2005 member states committed to Principle of Responsibility to protect. If a state is unwilling or unable to protect its population then that responsibility falls on international community and that humanitarian intervention will be through Security Council.

UNSC Reforms: The Challenge and the Prospects

Reforms in Security Council can be possible only through an amendment of Chapter 18 of UN Charter. (www.indiatoday.in, 2020) Charter amendment requires vote of two thirds of general Assembly members and must be ratified by two third members of the UN including all permanent members of the Security Council(Chapter XVIII, Article 108) (Mingst, 2010). Clearly, the current P-5 can act as "veto players" on UNSC reform. A similar mechanism can be identified, however, for other possible veto players. In this sense, nearly all UN regional groupings constitute almost a blocking minority. The distribution of vote shares in the UNGA for the five official regional groups clarifies that no reform of the UNSC is feasible without the consent of at least large parts of all regional groups. As shown in Table no. 3.3

Table 3.3: Membership of Regional Groupings in the United Nations (2014)

	Africa	Asia	Latin America and the Cari-bbean	Western Europe and Others	Eastern Europe	Total
Number of member states	54	53	33	29	23	192
Percentage of total UN membership	28.2	27.6	17.2	15.1	12.0	100

Source: https://digitallibrary.un.org/

Note: Total number of UN member states is 193; Kiribati is not member of any regional group. Africa includes South Sudan; Asia excludes Kiribati; Western Europe and Others includes the United States, Turkey and Israel. Due to rounding, percentages do not add up to exactly 100percent. Source: Calculations on the basis of UN data (un.org).

Table shows, the African group currently constitutes about 28.2percent of total UNGA membership. Similarly, the Asian group holds about 27.6percent. Accordingly, both of these regional groups are almost able to form a blocking minority. The other three regional groups "Latin America and the Caribbean" "Western Europe and Others" and "Eastern Europe" have a combined share of over 40 percent. Likewise, a combined share of almost 33 percent is reached by a coalition of the "Latin American and Caribbean" and the "Western Europe and Others" group. However, the Asian group with China, "Western Europe and Others" with France, the United Kingdom or the US, and finally, the Eastern European group with Russia, can veto any reform proposal, even when all other groups are united.

Hence, reform of the UNSC and any amendment to the UN Charter is a truly global enterprise that cannot be achieved if it lacks political will. Membership of regional groupings in the United Nations (2014) Africa Asia Latin America and the Caribbean Western Europe and Others Eastern Europe Total Number of member states 54 53 33 29 23 Percentage of total 192 UN membership i.e. 28.2 27.6 17.2 15.1 12.0 percent support in any of the regional groups.

In practice, the sponsors of each of the UNSC reform proposals aim to gather a large number of supporting nations, partially across the boundaries of the existing regional groupings. Hence, status quo bias as regards the potential for UNSC reform is affected by two major components:

(a) The existence of various veto players and

(b) Strongly increased institutional inertia over time. These factors explain why change is so difficult to effect in the framework of today's 193 member UNGA, constituting a major generally underestimated challenge to global diplomacy and to the negotiation skills of many who have aimed to render discussions on UNSC reform options a success.

Even the sophisticated tactics of Zahir Tanin, for example, who has been chairing the intergovernmental negotiations on UNSC reform, are largely ineffective in the face of the institution's inherent status quo bias. Without the decision-making rule that empowers the permanent members to veto a decision, a solution would certainly be more likely. For the other possible veto players, which hold at least one-third of the votes in the UNGA, only a solution that does not decrease their representation in relative terms will have a chance of success. But often, regional groupings themselves are not entirely cohesive in their preferences, largely due to internal rivalries about who might qualify to gain a seat in the UNSC, particularly between members of the G4 and UFC.

G4 nations called for a revamp of the UN Security Council on 23 Sept, 2020 to make it more representative, legitimate and effective of the current global order, to restore confidence in international cooperation and Global governance. Indian Government emphasised the need for expansion of the Security Council in both categories (permanent and non-permanent) to preserve its credibility and stopping it from becoming obsolete. G4 countries reiterated their support for each other's candidatures as aspiring new permanent members in reformed Security Council. Four Permanent members of UNSC support India i.e. Britain, France, Russia and the U. S. Only China opposed India (Roche, India,three other nations call for UN Security Council revamp, 2020).

In sum, the current reform proposals seem inadequate to ameliorate the flaws of the Security Council. Some might even make the situation worse. Reform efforts are being made but they are slow and incremental (Lattila, 2019). Because of demand for global governance the need for reforms in Security Council is required (Worsnip, 2009).

The UN Secretary-General Antonio Guterres in his address during his visit to India in September 2019 stressed "We are facing unprecedented challenges today, so we need to adapt and make the organisation fit for purpose. That is why I embarked on the reform of three key areas: the peace and security architecture, UN development system and management. I highly appreciate the support India has given to my reform proposals"

Prime Minister Narender Modi in his address at 12th BRICS summit 2020 via video-conferencing held on 16th November 2020 stated

"The world is seeing major geostrategic changes and effectiveness of global institutions are at stake and Reforms are required in IMF, WTO, WHO and Security Council India is a firm supporter of multilateralism and firmly committed to the values of the United Nations. During Covid time strength of India's pharmacy sector, helped over 150 countries by providing them medicines (Ghosh, 2020). Thus it can be concluded that reform does not start and begin with expansion of the Council and the addition of new categories of membership or additional permanent members. A host of working method reforms should also be considered."

President of the 75th session of the United General Assembly H.E. Mr. Volkan Bozkir, stated "It is crucial that any reforms to the Security Council reflect the realities of the 21st century." The implementation of the Council's decisions, and its very legitimacy, could be enhanced if the Council was reformed to be more representative, effective, efficient, accountable and transparent,"

Summary

This chapter discusses about the need for reforms in Security Council whose prime responsibility is for the maintenance of global peace and security and its decisions are binding for all member states. Its limited geographical balance combined with five exclusive permanent seats that have veto powers, however, makes the Security Council less representative than desired by many member states especially emerging 'middle' powers – and they are increasingly calling for a restructuring of the Council. A few permanent members use it as an instrument for justifying or imposing their policies and preferences which is contrary to the spirit of UN Charter. Thus the need for democratisation and enlargement of the Security Council is felt. Various Security Council reforms proposals e.g. Kofi Anan Proposal, Razali Proposal, Panama Innovative Proposal, The Two-Layered Regional Model have been discussed in detail. Claim of G4, L69, Coffee club, African Group, ACT, Arabic Group for Security Council reforms has been examined in this chapter. Various issues and challenges regarding Security Council reforms are also analysed. The chapter concludes that to make Security Council more representative, legitimate and effective in the current global order and to restore confidence in international cooperation and global governance reforms in Security Council is required. Indian Government emphasised the need for expansion of the Security Council in both categories (permanent and non-permanent) to preserve its credibility and in stopping it from becoming obsolete.

References

Abbi, R. (2017). *United Nations Organization Its role in Third World Countries.* New Delhi: The Readers Paradise.

Freiesleben, J. V. (2020, November 20). *Reforms in Security Council.* Retrieved from https://www.globalpolicy.org/images/pdfs/032008reform.pdf.

Ghosh, P. (2020, November 17). "Terrorism, Covid-19 Vaccine, Self Reliant India: What PM Modi said at 12th BRICS Summit 2020". *Hindustan Times.*

Harsh.V. Pant, H. S. (2020, September 18)." 75 years of UN-Need for Reforms" In Rajya Sabha Channel. (V. Dahiya, Interviewer)

India Today (2020, July 27). Retrieved from www.indiatoday.in.

Indian Express. (2020, September 22). *"UN and the New Multilateralism".*

J. Padelford, N. (1948). "The Use of the Veto". *International organization.*

Kelly-Kate. (2012). *International Organization (*Fifth Edition*).* London: Routledge,Taylor and Francis Group.

Lattila, V. (2019, May 28). "A New Proposal For UN Security Council Reform". *Oxford Research Group.*

Lavanya, R. (1995). *'Democratization of the United Nations'. Economic and Political Weekly,* New york.

Lewis, P. (1997, March 21)." U.N.Panel Proposes Expanding Security Council to 24 Members". *The New York Times.*

Mehrish, B. (2007). *The United Nations in the New Millennium : A Changing Scenerio.* Delhi: Academic Excellence.

Mingst, M.P. (2010). *International Organizations,The Politics and Processes of Global Governance.* New Delhi: Viva Books.

Nadin, P. (2014, August 23). Vision 2020: A Discussion of UN Security Council Reform. *Our World.*

Natalino, P.N. (2013). "The European Union and the Reform of the UN Security Council: Toward a new Regionalism?"

P. Saksena, K. (1993). *Reforming the United Nations The Challenge of Relevance.* California: Sage Publications.

Pease, K.K. S. (2012). *International Organizations.* London: Routledge.

Pramit Pal Chaudhary, F.A. (2020, September 18). "75 years of UN- Need for Reforms"Rajya Sabha Channel. (V. Dahiya, Interviewer)

Roche, E. (2020, September 23). "India,three other Nations call for UN Security Council Revamp". *mint.e paper.*

Saxena, S. (2020, September 16). "IBSA Calls for Speedy Global Efforts to Reform UN Security Council". *Hindustan Times.*

Stephen, S. (1997). "Can the United Nations Reform? ". *World Policy Journal.*

Worsnip, B. P. (2009, February 19). Reuter. "UN Launches Talk to Expand Security Council".

Zhenqiang, P. (2005). "On Reforms of the UN Security Council". *Online Info-Service Vol. 2/2005*

Chapter - 4

India's Claim for Permanent Seat in the Security Council

The Security Council is the single most watched issue within the country when it comes to the United Nations Organization. As the sanctum sanctorum and prime custodian of International Law, the Security Council has more powers than any other entity in the International System. India's concerted bid to be admitted as a veto-wielding permanent member of the Security Council is the single most watched issue within the country when it comes to the United Nations organization as a whole (Yadav, 2014).

In the Indian eyes "Reforms of the United Nations is incomplete without changing the composition of Security Council" (Nafey, 2005).The demand regarding India's inclusion in a reformed security council keeps getting shriller as the country persists with large personnel contribution to UN peacekeeping missions and leap frogs out of mediocre economic performance into an Asian giant with a Pluralistic Democratic Political System to boot" (Sreeram, 2009).

Understanding the Role of Security Council: Indian Experiences

The origins of the Indian interests in the Security Council can be traced back to the founding of the UN itself when Mahatma Gandhi felt that India, then including Pakistan and Bangladesh, should become a veto-wielding member of the Security Council (Stephen, 2001).Later,

India's first Prime Minister Jawaharlal Nehru shied away from the offer to join the Security Council by both the superpowers, the US and Soviet Union in 1950 and in 1955 respectively, keeping in mind the emerging Cold War calculus and steadfastly refused to join at the expense of China (Harder, 2017).

Nehru wrote: "It would do us little good and it would bring a great deal of trouble in India, because of many factors. India is certainly entitled to a permanent seat in the Security Council. But we are not going in at the cost of China (Murthy, 2017)." The UN Security Council, with its exceptional role in the UN in preserving international peace and security, has always been of significance for India right since its founding years (Murthy, 2011).

Case for Permanent Membership of India in UNSC

Indian tryst for permanent membership of Security Council flows broadly from following streams.

India as One of the Oldest Civilization

India is one of the oldest civilizations and has a vast experience and history of enriched culture and tradition. On the basis of rich cultural heritage India demands that it should be there in the Security Council as a permanent member.

Map 4.A: Ancient Civilization of Old World

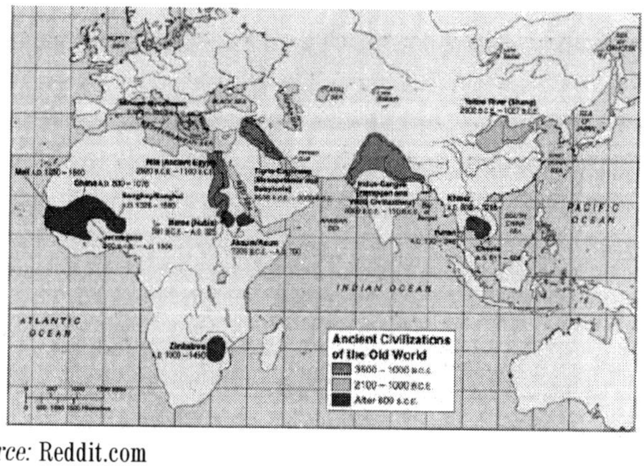

Source: Reddit.com

India's Historic Association with the UN System

India was among the members that signed United Nations Declaration on 1st January, 1942. India also had also the privilege to attend the historic UN Conference at San Francisco from 25 April to 26th June 1945. India as a founding and charter member of the United Nations has participated in all of its specialized agencies and organizations thus its claim for permanent membership of the United Nations gets strengthened.

First President of ECOSOC was an Indian

India has given its assistance to UN's development work from beginning. India played significant role in shaping ECOSOC agenda and always supported ECOSOC that was one of the six principal organs of the UN. The first meeting of ECOSOC was convened on January 23, 1946 in London. The President of ECOSOC was Sir Ramaswami Mudaliar from India.

India a Permanent Member of International Atomic Energy Agency

International Atomic Energy Agency is a specialized agency of United Nations. It is the nuclear watchdog of United Nations. India is a permanent member of the International Atomic Energy Agency and plays important role in its deliberations.

India's Intrinsic Value

India is the largest democracy and second-most populous country in the world. These are the primary reasons for India to be granted permanent membership in UNSC. India is a long standing democracy and an exemplar of liberal values. India has always taken the lead role in furthering universal good disarmament, climate accord and solar alliance.

India's Denial of UNSC Permanent Membership

In the past, India was informally offered to join the UNSC by both the superpowers, the US and the then Soviet Union in 1950 and in 1955 respectively, However, India denied the offer due to Cold War politics in that era.

India as a Non-Permanent Member

India was elected as a non-permanent member of the UNSC for eight terms, viz. in 1950 – 1951, 1967 – 1968, 1972 – 1973, 1977 – 1978, 1984 – 1985, 1991 – 1992, and 2011 – 2012 and 2020-2022. Thus after Japan Brazil and Argentina, India was elected the highest number of time as a non-permanent member of the Security Council.

Chart 4.1: No of Times Countries Elected to Security Council

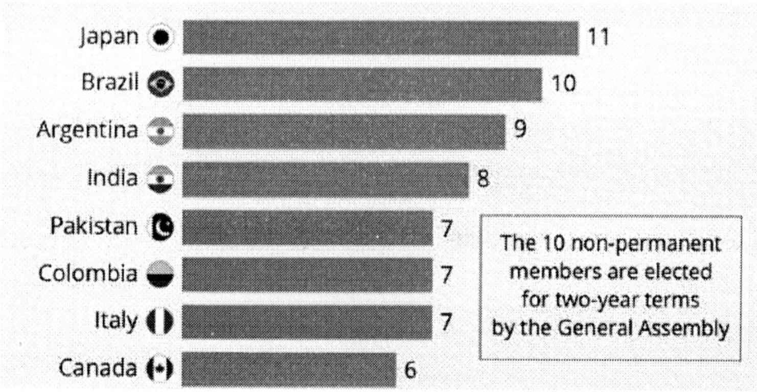

Source: www.un.org

Moreover India was elected as a non-permanent member of the Security Council eight times with an overwhelming support when member states elected India to the non-permanent seats and India got 184 out of the 192 valid votes polled for the term 2021-2022. This shows the faith of the countries in India's potential to lead in United Nations (Wire, 2020).

Unanimous Endorsement of the 55 Nation Asia- Pacific Group for India's Claim for Non-Permanent Seat in United Nations Security Council

It was a win-win situation for India when 55 states from Asia Pacific Group including China and Pakistan unanimously supported India for its claim for the non-permanent seat in United Nations Security Council in 2021-2022 for two years term.

Diplomatic Efforts of India in UN Security Council

India has served UN Security Council seven times and during each tenure India has given significant contribution. In 1950-51, India, as President of UNSC, presided over the adoption of resolutions calling for cessation of hostilities during the Korean War and for assistance to Republic of Korea.

In 1967-68, India co-sponsored Resolution 238 extending mandate of UN mission in Cyprus.

In 1972-73, India pushed strongly for admission of Bangladesh into UN. The resolution was not adopted because of a veto by a permanent member. In 1977-78, India was a strong voice for Africa in the UNSC and spoke against apartheid. Then External Affairs Minister Atal Bihari Vajpayee spoke in UNSC for Namibia's independence in 1978.In 1984-85, India was a leading voice in UNSC for resolution of conflicts in the Middle East, especially Palestine and Lebanon. In 1991-92, Prime Minister P V Narasimha Rao participated in the first ever summit-level meeting of the UNSC and spoke on its role in maintenance of peace and security. In 2011-2012, India was a strong voice for the developing world, peacekeeping, counter-terrorism and Africa. First statement on Syria was also given during India's Presidency at the UNSC.

During the 2011-12 term, India chaired the UNSC 1373 Committee concerning Counter-Terrorism, the 1566 Working Group concerning threat to international peace and security by terrorist acts, and Security Council 751/1907 Committee concerning Somalia and Eritrea.

India played an active role in discussions on all issues related to international peace and security, including several new challenges which the UNSC was called upon to deal with in Afghanistan, Cote d'Ivoire, Iraq, Libya, South Sudan, Syria and Yemen. In view of the threat posed to international trade and security by piracy off the coast of Somalia, India promoted international cooperation against the pirates.

At India's initiative, the Security Council mandated international cooperation for release of hostages taken by pirates as well as for prosecution of those taking hostages and those aiding and abetting these acts. India also worked for enhancing international cooperation in counter-terrorism, prevention of the proliferation of weapons of mass destruction to non-state actors.

Economic Potential of India as Criteria for Permanent Membership

India was the 5th largest economy and third largest in terms of purchasing power parity as of 2019 and one of the fastest-growing economies of the world. India's rising economic stature globally has added to Indian claims as well. However in the present scenario with the world reeling under the impact of pandemic, the Indian economy is expected to grow at 10.3 percent in 2020 as per the International Monetary Fund. India is expected to rebound in 2021 with 8.8 percent growth.

Table 4.1: Projected Growth of BRICS

BRIC Members	2020 (in percentage)	2021 (in Percentage)
India	-10.3	8.8
Russia	-4.1	2.8
China	1.9	8.2
South Africa	-8	3
Brazil	-5.8	2.8
World	-4.4	5.2

Source: World Economic Outlook October2020 Report

It is evident from analysis of the above Table that India's economy is projected to contract by 10.3 percent in 2020, the slowest among BRIC countries. The Table lists projections by IMF for 2020 and 2021 (The Hindu, 2020).Thus it can be analyzed that India's economy is expected to improve in 2021 and it will be able to contribute to world economy moreover its contribution to United Nations budget can be increased accordingly.

Centre for Economic and Business Research (U.K. Think tank) in its Report released on 26th December 2020 also forecasted that India's economy will expand by 9 percent in 2021 and 7 percent in 2022. India which was pushed back to World's sixth biggest economy due to the pandemic in 2020 will again overtake the U.K in 2025,Germany in 2027 and Japan in 2030 (Tribune, 2020).

India as a Software and IT Power

India's leading position in software and its IT-enabled services making it a global technology giant adds to its increasing economic and trade footprint across the world. India is now counted amongst the most influential players in economic organizations like the WTO, BRICS and the G20.

India as a Nuclear Weapon State

India's acquired status of a Nuclear Weapons State (NWS) in May 1998 also makes India a natural claimant as a permanent member similar to the existing. permanent members who are all Nuclear Weapon States.

India's Rising International Profile and Capabilities

India's international profile and capabilities are rising due to its ever-expanding global footprint in diverse areas like politics, sustainable development, economics, culture, science and technology. This can be seen in the proactive initiative pertaining to maritime and space diplomacy.

India's Induction into Export Control Regime

India was inducted to the Wassenaar Arrangement on 7 December 2017 as the 42nd member and recognized to have dual use technology. The fact that India was made a member of Wassenaar Arrangement even though it is not a signatory to the Nuclear NPT shows the strict adherence to non-proliferation that India has maintained. There is an exchange of notes when countries meet in such arrangements. India will gain access to high technology which will help address the demands of its defence and space sectors. (Dristi, 2020).

India Representing the Developing World

India is the undisputed leader of the Third world countries, as reflected by its leadership role in Non-Aligned Movement and G-77 grouping.

Population

India having a population of 1.28 billion will become the most populous country in the world in 2022. India as an independent country is a fairly young country at present although as a very ancient country it justifies "legitimate" candidature to be a permanent member of the UN Security Council (Shivam R., 2017).At the outset itself, demography remains the primary reason why India should be in the Council. India with its population at 1.28 billion now is the second most populous country in the world comprising almost one-fifth of humanity. This basic fact itself warrants Indian inclusion and representation in the Security Council. For India, moreover "population represents both an expression of the principle of democracy and an element of power. With increasing emphasis on the principle of democracy at the national level, there is a need for extending the principle to the international level also. "India has affirmed its willingness and capacity to shoulder the responsibilities of permanent membership. At the outset itself, demography remains the primary reason as shown in Chart 4.2 and that is why India should be in the Council.

Chart 4.2: World Population by Religion

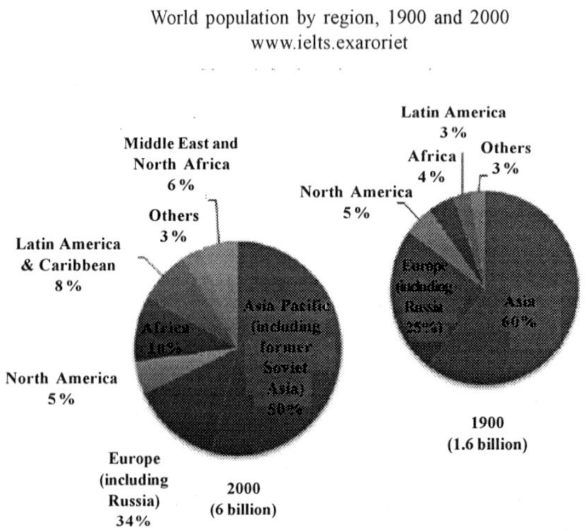

Source: Wikipedia

Map 4.B: World Population by Region

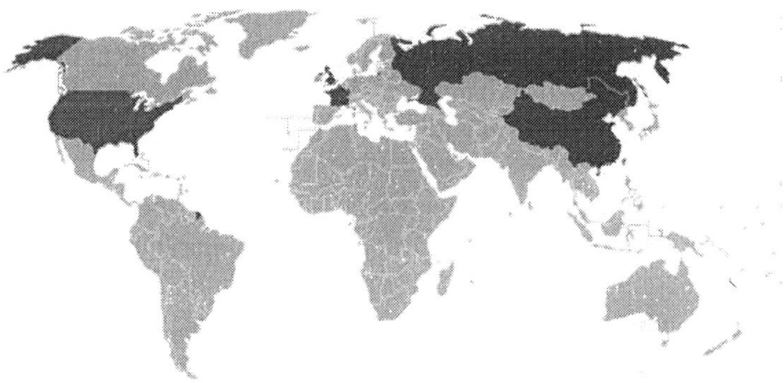

Source: Wikipedia

Above Graph predicts that Africa and Latin America has no representation, Asia is under presented and Europe in over Presented.

India as the Largest Democracy

India as the second most populous country, seventh largest country by land area is the most populous democracy in the world. India has always been ruled by democratic and secular Governments. India's largest democracy status is on the basis of being a country which has about 17.5 percent of the total humanity of the World. India has the largest electorate where elections are conducted in a free and fair manner by the Election Commission, a constitutional body under Article 324 elected Representative Act according to the constitution. India is the largest democracy of the world and its secular form is a message to the whole world about unity and integrity (Khan S. A., 2015).

India's Contribution in Environment Protection

As the world's fourth-largest emitter of carbon dioxide, India has been a central player in the negotiations of the two most recent climate change accords under the auspices of the UN. Indeed, India has described its own engagement, leading up to 15th Conference of the Parties (COP-15) in Copenhagen, as "taking initiative in facilitating international dialogue and discussion on critical climate change issues that are important for developing countries" (Jayaraman, 2009). In Paris, India was viewed as acting in a much more conciliatory manner, and willing to take on "a leadership role on climate negotiations" (Subramanian A. , 2015). India was recognized as a drafting author of the agreements and a leader within the Brazil-South Africa-India-China (BASIC) coalition, as well as the broader Group of 77 (G77) coalition at, Copenhagen and Paris Conferences of the Parties (COPs) (Kazmin, 2009). India has also advocated forcefully for the inclusion of the principle of "differentiation" in these accords (Ananthakrishnan, 2015). It "calls upon developed countries to absorb more stringent responsibilities in reducing carbon emissions than their developing country partners," which have been endorsed by India's partners in BASIC and the G77 (Science, 2020). The institutional framework of negotiations under the UNFCCC created a natural bias for an Indian alliance with its fellow members in BASIC, since member states in climate change negotiations are grouped into three "annexes" which separate developed economies from the developing ones (Keohane, 2014).In Paris, Prime Minister Narendra Modi of India introduced the concept of Climate Justice driving home the message of sustainable development" (Katju, 2015).

India's Ability to Work with all the Members

There is polarization among permanent members of Security Council where U.S., U.K and France are on one side while Russia and China are on another side. India has the ability that it can work well with all of them. India's participation in UN was notable for its efforts to resist the imposition of superpower disputes on UN General Assembly debates and its focus international attention on the problems of economic development (Mohanty, Foreign Policy of India in the 21 st century, 2017).

International Solar Alliance

India proposed International Solar Alliance (ISA), a multilateral alliance of 120 countries in support of "efficient exploitation of solar energy to reduce dependence on fossil fuels" (Neslen, 2015).In order to reduce footprints of carbon, India along with France has taken initiative to set up International Solar Alliance that is a growing organization with 88 signatories who will contribute in reducing carbon footprints.

Inspired by traditional ethos of living with environment have taken various initiatives, India had made LED lights popular and saved 38 million tons of carbon dioxide. Through Ujjwala scheme smoke free kitchens have been provided to 80 million households. India aims to restore 26 million hectares of degraded land by 2030 and will meet the goal of 175 Giga watts of renewable energy well before the target of 2022.

Coalition for Disaster Resilient Infrastructure

In order to increase resilience of critical infrastructure India has taken initiative to set up Coalition of Disaster Resilient Infrastructure. 18 countries including 9 from the G20 and four international organizations have joined this coalition. It is going to be helpful for poorer nations in due course of time (PIB, 2020).

India's Role during the Pandemic

Resilience of all the nations was tested during the COVID-19 pandemic. During the time of COVID-19 pandemic, India has extended medical and other assistance to more than 150 countries (ANI, 2020). UN chief Antonio Guterres also appreciated India's assistance to other countries to combat COVID-19 pandemic. The faith of the world towards India in the last six years has strengthened, whether it is FDI or FPI, foreign investors have made record investment in India during pandemic time. When the world is amid a health crisis in the form of Covid-19, India's vaccine diplomacy can be seen as opportunity to serve humanity and simultaneously strengthen its geopolitical position (Modi, 2015).

India as WHO Executive Head

WHO provides leadership to the entire world in the field of Public Health and has done so during this crucial period of pandemic. India was given the responsibility at a very challenging time. WHO executive board comprises of 34 members elected for three years term. The chair of the Executive Board is elected by its members on being nominated by the regional committee of WHO by rotation. Thus election of India as President shows the faith of the world community in India at the time of crisis. (Times, 2020).

Cooperation of India on Counter Terrorism

India has prioritized the adoption of an intergovernmental framework to combat terrorism (UN, 2020).To this end, India introduced the Comprehensive Convention on International Terrorism in 1996 (CCIT). India had some peripheral success in undertaking discussion linked to the CCIT which has led to the adoption of three separate protocols that aim to tackle terrorism (Livemint, 2016)

a) The International Convention for the Suppression of Terrorist Bombings, adopted on 15 December 1997;

b) The International Convention for the Suppression of the Financing of Terrorism, adopted on 9 December 1999; and

c) The International Convention for the Suppression of Acts of Nuclear Terrorism, adopted on 13 April 2005 (Livemint, "What Is the Comprehensive", 2012).

India is chairing three committees on Terrorism and is a leading voice in the UN in the fight against the global scourge of terrorism (mea.gov.in, 2015).

Counter Terrorism Committee: The committee was established after 9/11terror attack in United States and is working to bolster the ability of UN members to prevent terrorist acts both within their borders and across regions.

Taliban Sanction Committee: This Committee is also known as 1988 Sanction Committee. The Committee designates individuals and entities for participating in the financing, planning or perpetrating acts, supplying, selling and transferring arms, recruiting and supporting Taliban activities. The listed entities and individuals are subject to assets freeze, travel ban and arms embargo.

Libya Sanction Committee: Under the Committee all member states are required to prevent the sale or supply of arms, supply of funds, economic resources and related material to Libya.

UN Adopts two India Sponsored Resolutions on Nuclear Disarmament in 2020

The first committee of United Nations General Committee on November 03, 2020 adopted "Convention on Prohibition of the use of Nuclear Weapons" tabled by India since 1982 and Convention on "Reducing nuclear danger "under the nuclear weapon cluster" which was tabled by India since 1988. These resolutions manifest India's commitment towards the goal of nuclear disarmament (UN adopts India sponsored Resolutions on nuclear Disarmment, 2021).

India is the only Nuclear Weapon State that Demands for Total Elimination of Nuclear Weapons

India acquired the status of a Nuclear Weapons State in May 1998, although India has not been accorded de'jure recognition of this by the Nuclear Non Proliferation Treaty (NPT) of 1968. The Treaty was opened for signature in 1968 and entered into force in 1970. A total of 191 states have joined the Treaty. Four UN States have never accepted the NPT, three of which possess or are thought to possess nuclear weapons are India, Israel and Pakistan. In addition, South Sudan founded in 2011 has also not joined it. North Korea withdrew from the NPT in 2003 and has tested nuclear devices multiple times since 2006 despite international condemnation and sanctions. Year 2020 marked the 50th anniversary of the operationalization of the Treaty on the Non Proliferation of Nuclear Weapons.

India rejected Nuclear Non-proliferation Treaty as discriminatory saying it supports status quo of five existing nuclear power states. This demonstrates the paradox of India's commitment to multilateralism in nuclear disarmament, and at the same time, of it being a full-time nuclear weapons state (Das, 2016).India's nuclear doctrine at United Nations is in consonance with India's commitment to achieve global disarmament and maintain international peace and security. India always stands for total nuclear disarmament and its non-proliferation and elimination of weapons of mass destruction. India supports no first to use policy for nuclear weapons Later on India stands recognized as a de'facto NWS as a nuclear deal signed by India and U.S. A. in 2005 and nuclear supplier's waiver in 2008 regarding nuclear transfers for India despite not being an NPT signatory (Rajagopalan, 2015).

India is the only nuclear weapon state that demands for total elimination of nuclear weapons. At present India has a nuclear power generation capacity of 7.48 GW.

Table 4.2: Nuclear Power Plants in India

Power Station	State	Total capacity (MW)
Kaiga	Karnataka	880
Kakrapar	Gujarat	1140
Kudankulam	Tamil Nadu	2,000
Madras (Kalpakkam)	Tamil Nadu	440
Narora	Uttar Pradesh	440
Rajasthan	Rajasthan	1180
Tarapur	Maharashtra	1400
Total		7480

Source: Civil Services Chronicle, January 2021

In January 2015 India and United States released a joint statement that these two nations will work towards India's phased entry to nuclear suppliers group, Missile Technology Control Regime, The Wassenaar Arrangement and the Australian Group. As of 2018, India is a member of three of the four aforementioned regimes, and the NSG continues to be the sole holdout owing to Chinese opposition (Leveringhaus, 2017). The nuclear deals with multiple states also display the widespread recognition of India as a "responsible nuclear state (Ghoshal, 2018).

Chart 4.3: No. of Operational Reactor Units by the Country in 2019

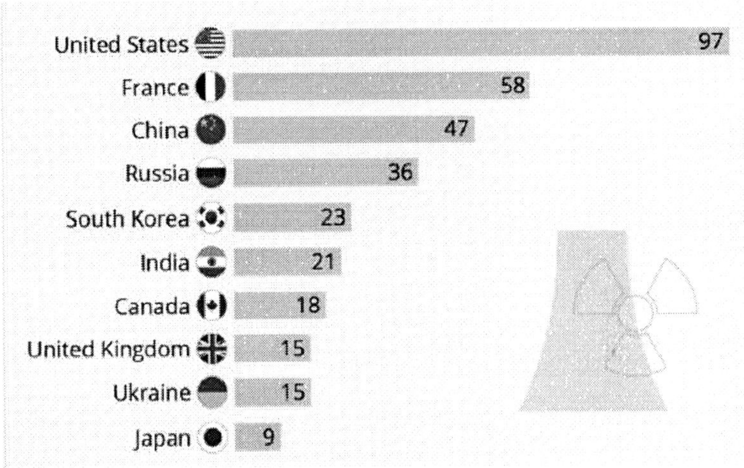

Source: World Nuclear Industrial Status Report 2019

India remained committed to "Universal, verifiable and non-discriminatory nuclear disarmament". India has now changed track to more conventional nuclear weapons state behaviour (PTI, "Committed to Non-Discriminatory", 2017).

India's Role in Peacekeeping

One of India's biggest contributions to global governance is its constant supply of able, highly skilled, and professional military forces to peacekeeping operations. India's large troop contribution does reinforce India's claim for a permanent seat when the UNSC is expanded. The term peacekeeping is not found in the UN Charter. Nevertheless, over the years, peacekeeping has come to be the most significant way in which the United Nations has fulfilled its responsibility to maintain international peace and security. Today, most significantly, India has almost twice the number of peacekeepers deployed on the ground as much as by P5 countries.

According to a United Nations Report, India is one of the founder members of the United Nations and has appreciated its responsibilities towards the United Nations Charter and consistently contributed towards United Nations efforts in maintenance of international peace and security. It may be noted that India's participation in United Nations Peacekeeping Operations started in 1950 and continues till date. In fact, India has earned the distinction of being amongst the longest serving and the largest troop contributors to the United Nations Peacekeeping activities.

India has contributed troops to United Nations peace keeping efforts in Korea, Egypt, Congo, Somalia, Angola, Haiti, Liberia, Lebanon, Rwanda and South Sudan conflict. India has taken part in 44 peacekeeping missions with 180,000 troops. India is also the third largest contributor of female police officers. United Nations has arrears of USD 38 million to India for its troops as on 16th April, 2019.

In the arena of peacekeeping, India is the largest contributor with 180,000 troops since 1950. Currently around 7700 Indian peacekeepers have been deployed in 13 missions in 11 countries out of total 16 missions (Permanent Mission of India,71st Session 2016, UN General Assembly: Background and Approach, 2016). A brief outline of India's peacekeeping mission in various countries is given below.

Korea

India's First peacekeeping assignment was in Korea when the 60 Para Field Ambulance of the Indian Army formed a part of the UN force under General Douglas MacArthur. The team performed lifesaving surgeries' and treated 400 casualties. The Indian handled the delicate situation with compassion, patience, fairness and neutrality, which earned them worldwide admiration.

Congo

In 1961 the Indian Army contributed an infantry brigade for conduct of military operations in Congo. This brigade successfully conducted the first peace enforcement operations of the United Nations. On 31 December, 1961 the Brigade Group regained full control of Katanga amidst stiff resistance by the Katangese Gendarmerie. By the end of 1962 the Indian brigade secured the key town of Kolwezi. On account of pressure of Indian brigade, the Gendarmerie laid down their arms which resulted in reunification of Congo.

Gaza

In 1956 India contributed infantry battalion of the United Nations Emergency Force (UNEF), which monitored the buffer zone between Egypt and the Anglo-French forces. The Indian contingent ensured smooth exchange of prisoners of war. It monitored the withdrawal of Israeli forces from the Sinai Peninsula and supervised the cession of hostilities between Egypt and Israel along the Armistice Demarcation line. The Indian peacekeepers maintained peace in the Gaza Strip till may 1967, when war again broke out between Egypt and Israel. In fact even at present an Infantry Battalion Group of India is performing the delicate task of maintaining peace in Southern Lebanon as part of UNIFIL.

Cambodia

India contributed infantry battalion group, field ambulance company, mine training teams, staff personnel and military observers to the United Nations Transitional Authority in Cambodia (UNTAC) to deal with the Cambodian crisis.

Somalia

India contributed to UNOSCOM II (United Nations Operations in Somalia) which sought to restore order, promote reconciliation and help rebuild Somalia's civil government and economy.

Namibia

India contributed contingents to the United Nations Transition Assistance Group (UNTAG) which was formed to ensure free and fair elections in Namibia (formerly known as South West Africa).

Rwanda

In addition to the above discussed operations, India also contributed peacekeeping contingent to United Nations Assistance Mission for Rwanda (UNAMIR), which was set up to monitor implementation of the Agreement and assist in the establishment and maintenance of a transitional government in Rwanda.

Angola

India also contributed contingents to the United Nations Angola Verification Mission (UNAVEM) which was dispatched to Angola to monitor the Cuban troop's withdrawal. This withdrawal was completed in May 1991.

Sierra Leone

In October 1999, India in pursuance of UN Security Council Resolution, contributed two infantry battalions, Aviation Units and support elements to the United Nations Peacekeeping Mission in Sierra Leone (UNAMSIL). However in view of the hostilities by the Revolutionary United Front (RUF) 221 Indian peacekeepers and military observers had to live under siege, which they faced with great courage. This was greatly commended by the UN as well as the world media.

Lebanon

In 1998 India contributed an infantry battalion comprising of 619 ranks to the UN Interim Force in Lebanon (UNIFIL) which was established in 1978 after occupation of Southern Lebanon by Israel. Subsequently India contributed another 172 troops to this force. The Indian soldiers played an important role in checking sporadic incidents of violence between the Israel Defence Forces and Hezbollah group.

Kosovo

India also participated in the UN Peacekeeping Mission in Kosovo (UNMIK) and contributed 300 civilian police officers. In addition, it deployed two companies comprising of 240 personnel. India also deputed 30 Indian civil servants, who helped in the management of civil administration in Kosovo. The Indian contingent earned great admiration for its discipline and professionalism from various quarters.

India as Military Observer to Central America ONUCA (89-92) and El Salvador (91-95)

India has also contributed military observers to peacekeeping operations in Central America ONUCA (89-92) and El Salvador (91-95).

Induction of India into Missile Technology Control Regime

It is an informal and voluntary partnership among 35 countries to prevent the proliferation of missile and unmanned aerial vehicle technology capable of carrying greater than 500 kg payload for more than 300 km. It was established in April 1987 by G-7 countries USA, UK, France, Germany, Canada, Italy, and Japan. India was inducted into the Missile Technology Control Regime in 2016 as the 35th member. India has joined MTCR as a full member and also agreed to join the Hague Code of conduct which bolstered its position as a responsible nuclear state and strengthen its case for the membership of Nuclear Suppliers Group. India can procure high-end missile technology and run joint programmes for development of unmanned aerial vehicles with other countries e.g. Procurement of theatre missile interceptor "Arrow II " from Israel, military drones like "Avenger" from the USA etc.

Induction of India to the Wassenaar Arrangement

India was inducted to Wassenaar Arrangement on 7 December, 2017 as the 42nd member implies that India is also recognised to have dual use technology. There is an exchange of notes when countries meet in such arrangements. So, India will gain access to high technology which will help to address the demands of its defence and space sectors (Dristi, 2020).

India's Contribution to the UN: Acknowledgements

India has always seen itself as a champion, a 'moralistic force' of the so called Third World, the developing states. Former Secretary General, Kofi Annan has been quoted as saying that India has been one of the most significant votaries of shaping the UN agenda on behalf of the developing world. But even more significantly, the effectiveness of such participation and commitment to United Nations peacekeeping efforts has drawn respect and praise from fellow professionals of other countries and many others that have served jointly with our commanders, observers, police monitors and contingents, in various parts of the world. Hence, the image of the Indian armed forces and police in the international arena is that of highly competent, professional, and well-trained forces.

In 2001, the then UN Secretary General Kofi Annan singled out our peace keepers for special praise and told them, "You have much to teach the peace keepers of other countries, who may share your enthusiasm and determination, but lack your experience and training". Thus on the basis of above discussion it can be concluded that India has to display more pragmatism to realize its aspiration to be a permanent member of Security Council (Schaffer, 2010).

Indian Strategies: Diplomacy in Action

India has adopted a multi-layered strategy to assume the highly coveted permanent seat in the Security Council. According to Stuenkel, the Indian strategy of "revisionist integration" into the Security Council consists of two components:

1) Maximizing support in the UN General Assembly

2) Minimizing resistance in the UN Security Council

Challenges Before Permanent Membership of India

Less Financial Contribution of India to United Nations

India's financial contribution to United Nations is less as compared to other countries as shown in following graph.

Graph 4.1: India's Contribution to UN Regular Budget from 2013-2019

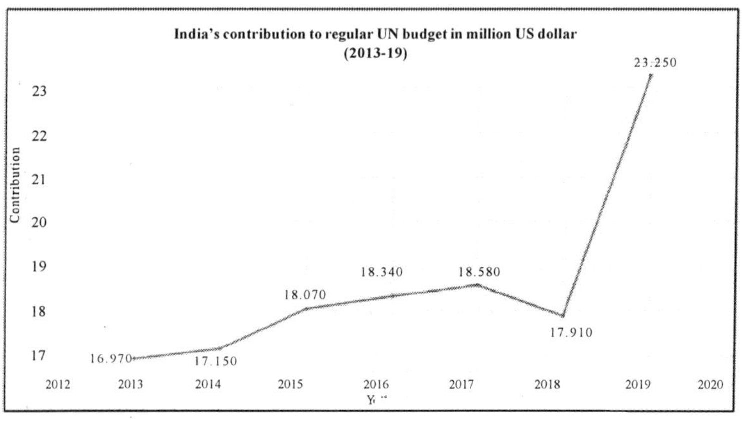

Source: https://digitallibrary.un.org/

India's contribution to the UN regular budget was $16.97 million in 2012-13, $17.19 million in 2013-14, $18.07 million in 2014-15 and $18.58 million in 2017. India's actual share in 2019 was $25.5 million dollars, but is given a credit of $2.3 million for the income tax exemption extended by India for the UN staff working in India. Hence, the net share of India's contribution is $23.25 million. There is a sharp increase in 2019 because of the increase in the share of India's contribution for 2019-21 cycles.

Graph 4.2: India's Total Contribution to UN in INR (Annual Budget 2010-2019)

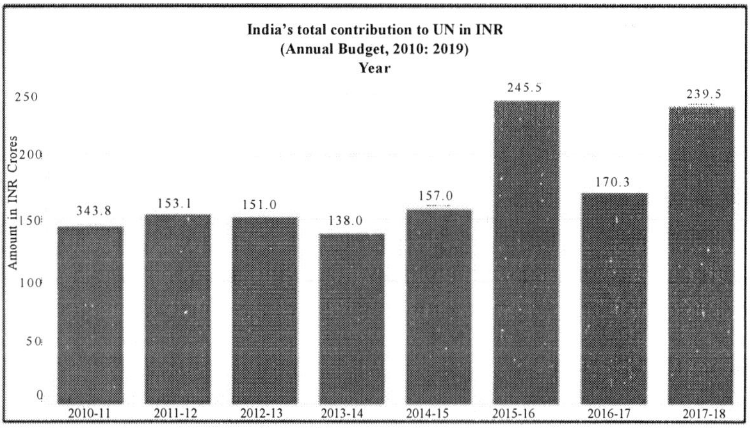

Source: www.un.org

India's total contribution to the UN (including for all UN agencies) was Rs. 138 Crore in 2013-14, Rs. 157 Crore in 2014-15, Rs. 244 Crore in 2015-16, Rs. 170.28 Crore in 2016-17 and Rs. 239.47 Crore in 2017-18. This has been illustrated in the following graph. It is clearly visible that India's highest contribution was in the financial year 2015-16 followed by 2017-18.India is a regular contributor to UN's budget. For Financial year 2015-2016, India's contribution was Rs. 2,440,000,000 (US $34 million) which was 55 percent more than the previous year.

According to the assessment made for the years 2019-21, India has to contribute 0.83percent to the UN regular budget, up from 0.73percent during the 2016-18 period. India's share in global GNP is now around 2.77percent. This has resulted in India becoming the 21st largest contributor as compared to 24th position in the previous assessment cycle. There is an 8.8 percent increase in India's contribution. Based on the assessment by the contributions committee, India's contribution to the UN regular budget was fixed at 0.53percent for 2009-12 and 0.66percent for 2013-2015.

India also contributed to the other UN agencies like the UNDP, UNICEF, and UNEP etc. India's contribution to UN peacekeeping operations was fixed at 0.106percent for the period 2009-12 and at 0.133percent for the period 2013-15 and 0.147 percent for the period 2016-18. For the period 2019-21, it has been fixed at 0.166percent. The total peacekeeping budget of the UN for 2019-20 is $6.51 billion. Among the BRICS nations, India's contribution is more than only South Africa. Brazil, Russia and China contribute more than India to the UN budget.

Thus, India's contribution is quite less as compared to developed countries. Those nations which are contributing more than India can block the permanent membership of India in the Security Council.

Institutional Inertia: Path Dependency and Veto Players

Veto players are actors required for changing the status quo or conversely, without their consent, no institutional change is achievable. The configuration of veto players is set up by the constitutional provisions that give rise to the structure of an institution. Therefore, the prospect of successfully changing the status quo relies on the number of veto players and their preferences toward a new policy.

Bargaining, Inertia and Blocking Power

In order to change the size, composition, veto privileges and majority threshold applicable to the UNSC, notably to make it more representatives of current global power distributions, the UN Charter text of articles 23 and 27 would need to be amended. To achieve this, these provisions, like any other in the UN Charter could be altered by adopting a UNGA resolution (UN Charter Art. 108) or by first convening a "General Conference" of all UN Members "for the purpose of reviewing the present Charter," which then could recommend an "alteration" of the Charter text corresponding to a UNGA resolution (UN Charter art. 109). In essence, both provisions require a comprehensive formal agreement by a two-thirds majority and subsequent ratification by two-thirds of the UNGA, as well as the permanent members of the UNSC. To date, however, the composition of the UNSC has been amended only once increasing its membership from 11 to 15 according to the provisions of Article 108, while Article 109 has never been applied. With a total number of 193 member states, the two-thirds majority threshold in the UNGA (i.e. about 67percent of total UNGA membership), amounts to 129 votes; accordingly, a blocking minority can be formed by 65 states (i.e. about 33percent of the total).In such situation possibility of blocking of India's membership in UNSC can be there.

Challenge of Politics within UNSC

The seven previous terms have given Indian diplomats the experience of how diplomacy is conducted at the multilateral setting.

Chinmaya R Gharekhan, India's Permanent Representative at the UN during the 1991-1992 UNSC stint, wrote in his book "The Horseshoe Table" that the five permanent members would like the non-permanent members to be "cooperative", and not stand in the way of major resolutions. Most non-permanent members get influenced by the P-5 members. Gharekhan wrote, "They did not wish to irritate the permanent members, and were keen to be perceived by them as 'cooperative'. This was precisely how the permanent members would like the non-permanent members to behave. The Indians took their work more seriously, and consequently had to fight a lonely battle." This was the time when the Gulf War erupted and India voted in favour of the US-sponsored resolution in April 1991.

"India's vote was dictated by pragmatic considerations. The Americans had made it clear to India, in Washington as well as in New Delhi, that failure to support the resolution would make it very difficult for them to help India in the World Bank and the IMF," Gharekhan wrote. India was going through a severe balance-of-payment crisis, and needed funds from these organizations. Also, India needed the US on its side, if and when the Kashmir issue came up. Thus, challenge of politics within the UNSC is the biggest block before the permanent membership of India.

The China Challenge

India is entering the UNSC at a time when Beijing is asserting itself at the global stage much more vigorously than ever. It heads at least six UN organizations and has challenged the global rules. China's aggressive behaviour in the Indo-Pacific as well as the India-China border has been visible in entire 2020. At Pakistan's behest; China has tried to raise the issue of Kashmir at the UNSC but has not found much support. There is some discussion among the strategic community for raising the issues of Taiwan, Hong Kong and Tibet at the UNSC. But, the polarizing politics inside India gives a window of opportunity to its rivals, and opens up the possibility of criticism especially on human rights issues (Roy, 2021).

India as a Nuclear Weapon State

India's acquired status of a Nuclear Weapons State (NWS) in May 1998 also made India a natural claimant as a permanent member similar to the existing permanent members who are all Nuclear Weapon States. Security Council condemned the nuclear Tests conducted by India and urged India to become party to the Non Proliferation of the Nuclear Weapons (NPT) and to the Comprehensive Test Ban Treaty. China has been the biggest impediment to India gaining membership of the Nuclear Suppliers Group (NSG) and the United Nations Security Council (UNSC).

Blocking of India's Induction to Nuclear Suppliers Group

Nuclear Supplier Group (NSG) was formed in 1974 is comprised of 48 states that have voluntarily agreed to coordinate their export controls to non-nuclear weapon states. Current guidelines of NSG state that a non NPT state cannot become member of NSG. Ever since India applied for the membership of NSG in May 2016, China has been insisting that only those countries which have signed the NPT can join this group. Along with China, New Zealand, Ireland and Australia are also opposing Indian membership to Nuclear Suppliers Group on the basis of NPT non signatory status of India. China to further obstruct India's membership demand, had clubbed India's membership bid with that of Pakistan's. However, Pakistan's credentials for membership are extremely inaccurate. India is facing both domestic and political issues, and the challenges of working within a disorderly fragmented international scene. In such a situation sailing in the council will not be smooth.

India's Refusal to Sign the Comprehensive Test Ban Treaty

The 1998 nuclear test changed the nature of India's opposition to the CTBT. India is unlikely to be willing to participate in the CTBT in the event of a UNSC resolution.

Opposition by Uniting for Consensus (UFC) Group

Italy and Pakistan-led Uniting for Consensus (UFC) group firmly opposes any additional permanent members, saying that such a move will not make the body more effective and will also undermine the fundamental principle of democracy that is based on periodic elections.

Kashmir Issue

In the present scenario, existing confrontation between India and Pakistan on the Kashmir issue where India's proclamation has not been accepted by the UN, which continues to list Kashmir as disputed territory and subject to Security Council's self-determination resolutions in such situation permanent membership of India in Security Council can be at stake.

On 5th August 2019, the Government of India (GoI) announced the abrogation of Article 370 of the Constitution and the bifurcation of the state of Jammu and Kashmir (J&K) into two union territories. This triggered an unprecedented international response as though most countries agreed that the changes in Jammu and Kashmir were India's "internal matter" and differences should be resolved through dialogue between India and Pakistan. The SAARC countries of Bhutan, Bangladesh, Maldives, Nepal, Sri Lanka and Afghanistan have supported India's move on Article 370 and the bifurcation of the state (Kapoor, 2019).Tehran has maintained a restrained position on the developments in J&K since August 2019, and has avoided any confrontation with either nation. ("Iran urges India, Pakistan to resort to 'dialogue, peaceful methods' amid Kashmir tensions", 2019). Moscow has fully supported India's actions in J&K, stating that the decision was carried out within the framework of the Indian Constitution. ("Article 370: US urges all stakeholders to maintain peace, stability along LoC",, 2019).The abrogation of Article 370 initially evoked a muted reaction from the US, later it urged "all parties to maintain peace and stability along the Line of Control," (Parker, 2019).

However, some of India's strategic partners and longstanding friends have expressed concerns and criticized the communication clampdown, the detention of political leaders and the restriction of civil liberties. This can also impact India's claim for the UNSC seat. The Foreign Ministers of the OIC Contact Group on Kashmir later released a statement expressed its concerns regarding the situation in Kashmir and asked India to "rescind" the actions it had taken (PTI, 2019).

Islamabad made numerous attempts to get the UNSC to hold a discussion on Kashmir, but was unable to make progress until China stepped in. As a permanent member of the council and an ally of Islamabad, Beijing requested a "closed consultation" on Kashmir ("Kashmir Issue: Pakistan Gets Closed-Door Meeting at UNSC after China Steps In", 2019). UNSC discussing the Kashmir question for the first time since 1965 was a victory in itself, according to Pakistan, which projects itself as a champion for Kashmiri rights (Roche, "At UNSC, China and Pakistan Fail to Censure India over Article 370", 2019). However, Pakistan and China failed to get the international community to support their stand on Kashmir. No unanimous statement in favour of Beijing and Islamabad emerged from consultations at the UNSC, and the move to censure India fell through. Islamabad's ambassador to the US has gone so far as to link Kashmir with the US led peace process in Afghanistan, stating that Islamabad may be forced to redirect troops from the Afghan border to the Kashmir frontier (Gladstone, 2019). Imran Khan's opinion piece in The New York Times criticized the Government of India(GoI) and called the removal of Article 370 "illegal" (Khan I. , 2019). China's response to the changes in Kashmir focused on its concern over Ladakh becoming a Union

Territory. It called the move "unacceptable," claiming that it would directly "impede China's sovereignty" (Hua, 2019).

China's statements suggest that its opposition to the removal of Article 370 is driven by a fear that it would further complicate its boundary issue with India, in light of the 740-km LOC in J&K (PTI, Article 370, 2019). However, China soon revised its statement, stating that the Kashmir issue should be resolved bilaterally in a peaceful manner and that both sides must avoid any action that could escalate tensions in the region ("China 'Seriously Concerned' over Situation in Jammu and Kashmir", 2019).

During a China–Pakistan meeting in Beijing, the Chinese Foreign Minister said the solution should be in accordance with the UN Charter and relevant UNSC resolutions (PTI, "Ahead of Xi Jinping's Visit, China Says Kashmir Issue Should Be Resolved Bilaterally,", 2019).

After Pakistan transferred control of the Shaksgam Valley (northwest of the Siachen glacier) to China, giving it control over part of Pakistan-Occupied Kashmir (POK), China gained closer access to India's northern and western border (Bhatt, "Revisiting China's Kashmir policy", 2019).China's state-owned Xinhua quoted Xi as saying, "The dragon and elephant dance is the only correct choice for China and India" (Dutta, 2019). Indian media reports note that Xi mooted the idea of a trilateral partnership between Beijing, New Delhi and Islamabad (Aneja, 2019). This could be interpreted as China's effort to insert itself in matters concerning India and Pakistan, particularly vis-à-vis the J&K issue.

Beijing's interests in Jammu and Kashmir are both strategic and economic. In 2010, China started issuing stapled visas to the residents of J&K, manifesting its desire to cement its pro-Pakistan stance. The crown head of the Belt and Road Initiative (BRI), the China-Pakistan Economic Corridor (CPEC) runs through parts of POK. The sovereignty of this part is disputed, as India has repeatedly claimed the territory as its own. Recent statements from top ministers of the GoI have made it clear that the government will make efforts to take control of POK, which directly impinges upon China's interests in the region. The latter's US$19-billion investment in CPEC is directly linked to the Indo-

Pak territorial dispute over J&K, which will be affected by the balance of power shifting towards India (Ghosal, 2019).

Challenge of Post Covid Global Order

Global economy is in shambles with various countries facing recession and health emergencies. At the same time narrow nationalism is sweeping across the world which challenges the prospects of global cooperation. To handle all these situations need careful strategy to move the world out of this burdening challenge. With the situation deteriorating between USA and Russia and increasing tension between USA and Iran, it will be difficult situation for India to promote multilateral solutions to global problems.

Joe Biden Administration Changed Stand on India's Bid for Permanent Membership of UNSC

The U.S. has supported India's permanent membership to UNSC with Barack Obama declaring his country's support in his address to Parliament in 2010.In 2017, former U.S. President Donald Trump reaffirmed the U.S.'s support India's claim in a joint communiqué issued during Prime Minister Narendra Modi's visit to the White House. "Recognizing India's growing role in the world stage, the Obama-Biden Administration formally declared U.S. support for India's membership in a reformed and expanded United Nations Security Council," in Biden Campaign's policy document on Indian Americans. (The Hindu, 2021).Joe Biden's UN Ambassador nominee Linda Thomas-Greenfield remarked that India's bid for the permanent membership of UNSC was a 'matter of discussion" where Coffee Club countries opposing India's membership and on the other hand countries like Italy, Pakistan, Mexico and Egypt have also opposed permanent membership bid of India, Japan, Germany and Brazil. Thus changed stand of Biden administration can be challenge for permanent membership of India in UNSC.

Conclusion

India has emerged as a foremost, singularly acknowledged rising power seen by most states, great and small, as making a legitimate claim to a place in the changing architecture of global governance, including the UN Security Council. Successive Indian leaderships have therefore, emphasized time and again, the pressing need to democratize the international relations embodied in the UN and its all-powerful Security Council. The Indian decision makers realize that it is now historically placed to become an international rule maker and shaper, as opposed to a meek rule follower in the policy relevant future. It truly marks a rising India's dramatic desire to move to the centre from the periphery of global politics. When India is celebrating 75 years of India's independence, inclusion of India as a permanent member of Security Council will definitely add to its celebration and will be remembered as the year of pride and achievement.

To strengthen UN system to combat new global challenges such as terrorism, piracy, disarmament, peace building, peace keeping and Human Rights India can play effective role as permanent member of Security Council.

Swami Vivekananda has Rightly Said:

> "India for thousands of years peacefully existed even earlier when history has no records and tradition dare not peer into gloom of that intense past, even from then until now ideas after ideas have marched out from her, but every word have been spoken with a blessing behind it and peace before it. We, of all nations of the World have never been a conquering race and that blessing is on our head and therefore we live."

This message is still relevant in our quest to claim permanent membership in United Nations Security Council.

References

Abbi, R. (2017). *United Nations OrganizationIts Role in Third World Countries.* New Delhi: The Readers Paradise.

Ananthakrishnan, G. (2015, DECEMBER 9). "BASIC Optimistic About Legally Binding Paris Deal". *The HINDU.*

Aneja, A. (2019, October 16). "Xi Mooted Trilateral Partnership with Pakistan". *The Hindu.*

ANI News (2019, August). "China 'Seriously Concerned' over Situation in Jammu and Kashmir".

ANI. (2020, July 18). "India has Extended Assistance to over 150 Countries in Fight Against COVID-19 : PM Modi". *Health World.*

Batra, T. S. (1979). *The Security Council & Veto.* Delhi: B.V.Gupta Publishers.

Batra, T. S. (1979). *The Security Council & Veto.* New Delhi: Metropolitan Book Co. Pvt. Ltd.

Bhatt, P. (2019, November). "Revisiting China's Kashmir policy",. *ORF Issue Brief No. 326.*

Bhola, P. (2001). *Foreign Policies of India,Pakistan & China.* Delhi: RBSA Publishers.

Bhola, P. (2001). *Foreign Policies of India,Pakistan & China.* S.M.S. Highway, Jaipur: RBSA Publishers.

Bilgrami, S. J. (2004). *Dynamics of Sanctions in World Affairs.* New Delhi : Atlantic Publishers & Distributors.

Business Today. (2019, August 15) "Kashmir Issue: Pakistan Gets Closed-Door Meeting at UNSC after China Steps In".

Bussemaker, N. (2020, september 16). *https://www.cfr.org/backgrounder/un-security-council.* Retrieved November 19, 2020, from UN Security council: https://www.cfr.org/backgrounder/un-security-council

C.K. Webster. (1933). *The League of Nations in Theory and Practice,.* London : George Allen and Unwin Ltd.

Chunying', F. M. (2019, August 6). " Remarks on the Indian Government's Announcement of the Establishment of the Ladakh Union Territory Which Involves Chinese Territory".

Cilliers, J. (2015, April 8). "Does the UN Security Council need Reform?" *World Economic Forum.*

Civil Service Chronicle (2021, January). UN adopts India Sponsored Resolutions on Nuclear Disarmment.

Correspondent, L. (2016, September 28). "What Is the Comprehensive Convention on International Terrorism ?" *Livemint.*

Das, D. (2016, June 10). *http://www.catchnews.com/international-news/india-smembership-in-the-nsg-is-symbolic-lack-of-success-does-it-no-harm-*

1465552409.html. Retrieved December 2, 2020, from Catch News: http://www.catchnews.com/international-news/india-smembership-in-the-nsg-is-symbolic-lack-of-success-does-it-no-harm-1465552409.html.

Davydov, A. (2020). "China - USA -Russia: Geopolitics and Pandemic". *Far Eastern Affairs is a quarterly journal of the Institute for Far Eastern Studies Issue 2.*

Dristi (2020, March 4).

Duane, S. (2002). *Global Capital,Political institutions & Policy changes in Developed Welfare States.* Cambridge,U.K: Cambridge University Press.

Dutta, P. K. (2019, October 14). "Is There a Hidden Chinese Message in Modi-Xi Jinping Meet?". *India Today.*

Fies, H. (1957). *Churchill Roosevelt Stalin: The War they Waged and the Peace.* New Jersey.

Freiesleben, J.V. (2020, November 20). *Reforms in Security Council.* Retrieved from https://www.globalpolicy.org/images/pdfs/032008reform.pdf.

General, R.O. (2005). "In Larger Freedom: Towards Development, Security and Human Rights for all ". http://www.globalpolicy.org/images/pdfs/ followupreport.pdf.

General, U.N. (2017, May 1). *https://www.un.org/sg/en/content/sg/statement/2005-04-28/secretary-generals-public-lecture-india-international-centre-larger.* Retrieved December 5, 2020, from UNITED NATIONS: 28/secretary- generals-public-lecture-india-international-centre-larger

Geneva., I.C. (1940). International Consultative Group of Geneva. *'Causes of the Peace Failure' 1919-1939.*

Ghosal, A. (2019, August 30). "What Chinese Discourse Reveals about Beijing's Reaction to Article 370", *South Asian Voices.*

Ghosh, P. (2020, November 17). "Terrorism, Covid-19 Vaccine, Self-Reliant India: What PM Modi said at 12th BRICS Summit 2020". *Hindustan Times.*

Ghoshal, D. (2018, Feb 3). *https://scroll.in/article/867260/while-no-one-was-watching-india-worked-to-position-itself-as-a-responsible-nuclear-powered-nation.* Retrieved December 2, 2020, from Scroll: https://scroll.in/article/867260/while-no-one-was-watching-india-worked-to-position-itself-as-a-responsible-nuclear-powered-nation.

Gladstone, R. (2019, August 12). "Pakistan's Envoy Suggests Kashmir Crisis could Affect Afghan Peace Talks". *The New York Times.*

Gulati, S., Pal, A. & Bansal, A. (2020)." Fuzzy Evaluation of Impact of Lockdown Amid Corona Virus on Delhi's Pollution". *Advances in Mathematics: Scientific Journal.*

Harder, A. (2017, june 1). *https://www.wilsoncenter.org/publication/not-the-cost-china-india-and-the-united-nations-security-council-1950.* Retrieved november 28, 2020, from unsc: https://www.wilsoncenter.org/publication/not-the-cost-china-india-and-the-united-nations-security-council-1950

Harsh.V. Pant, H. S. (2020, September 18). "75 years of UN-Need for Reforms" In Rajya Sabha Channel. (V. Dahiya, Interviewer)

Herzog, S. (1999). "Globalization & Povert Allevation in India". *Liberal Times 3/99.*

Hindu, T. (2020, March27). "UN Security Council yet to Discuss Coronavirus Crisis under China's Presidency". *The Hindu.*

Hua, C. F. (2019, August 6). " Remarks on the Indian Government's Announcement of the Establishment of the Ladakh Union Territory Which Involves Chinese Territory".

India, M. O. (Annual Report: 2014-2015, 170, Annual Report: 2014-2015, 170 Annual Report: 2014-2015, 170). *http://www.mea.gov.in/Uploads/PublicationDocs/25009_External_Affairs_2014*-ExternalAffairs(2015*).2015__English_.pdf.* Retrieved December 1, 2020, from Ministry of External Affairs of India: http://www.mea.gov.in/Uploads/PublicationDocs/25009_External_Affairs_2014-2015__English_.pdf.

India, M.O. (2016, OCT 1). *http://www.mea.gov.in/Uploads/PublicationDocs/26525_26525_External_Affairs_English_AR_2015-16_Final_compressed.pdf.* Retrieved December 1, 2020, from Ministry of External Affairs of India: http://www. mea.gov.in/Uploads/PublicationDocs/26525_ 26525_External_Affairs_English_AR_2015-16_Final_compressed.pdf.

Indian Express. (2020, September 22). "UN and the New Multilateralism".

IndiaToday (2020, July 27).

Interview, C. (2017, March 26). "Permanent Mission of India to the United Nations in New York". (C. Interview, Interviewer)

J. Padelford, N. (1948). "The Use of the Veto". *International organization.*

Jayaraman, T. (2009, November 26). "India's Strategy at Copenhagen". *The Hindu.*

Johnson, T. (2010). *https://www.cfr.org/backgrounder/four-nuclear-outlier-states.* Retrieved December 2, 2020, from Crfonline: https://www.cfr.org/backgrounder/four-nuclear-outlier-states.

Joshi, M. (2020, November 10). "Biden's China Policy". *The Tribune.*

Kapoor, N. (2019, September 4). "Scrapping of Special Status to J-K is India's Internal Matter: Bhutan". *ANI News.*

Kapstein, E. B. (2000). "Winners & Losers in Indian Economy". *International Organizations, Vol.54, No.2 Spring,* 359.

Katju, V. (2015, JAN 31). "Working of External Affairs Ministry Needs Much Reform". *The Economic Times.*

Kazmin, A. (2009, December 22). "India Welcomes Copenhagen Accord". *Financial Times.*

Kelly-Kate. (2012). *International Organization (*Fifth Edition*).* London: Routledge, Taylor & Francis Group.

Keohane, R.O. (2014). "Multilateralism: An Agenda for Research". *International No 45,* no. 4 (Fall 1990): 731-46.

Khan, I. (2019, August 30). "Imran Khan: The World Can't Ignore Kashmir. We Are All in Danger". *New York Times.*

Khan, S.A. (2015, August 14). "Why India deserves a fixed UN Security Council Seat". *Politics.*

Knight, W.A. (2003). "The Future of the UN Security Council :Questions of Legitimacy & Representation in Multilateral Governance". In R. T. Andrew F. Cooper.John English, *Enhancing Global Governance* (pp. 19-37). Delhi: Book well.

Kohli, A. (2006). "Politics of Economic Growth in India 1980-2005" -Part II: The 1990 & Beyond. *Economic & Political Weekly.*

Krishnan, V. B. (2019, January 12). "India has Lost Highest Number of Personnel in UN Peacekeeping Mission". *The Hindu.*

Lattila, V. (2019, May 28). "A New Proposal For UN Security Council Reform". *Oxford Research Group,* pp. 1-3.

Lavanya, R. (1995). "Democratization of the United Nations ". *Economic and Political Weekly,*New york.

Leland, M. G. (1972). "The UNITED NATIONS ". New York: The Free Press.

Leveringhaus, K. S. (2017, June 30). "China's stance on NSG Membership Shows the Extent of India's Challenge in the Global Nuclear Order". *The Wire.*

Lewis, P. (1997, March 21)." U.N.Panel Proposes Expanding Security Council to 24 Members". *The NewYork Times.*

Livemint. (2012). "What Is the Comprehensive".

Livemint. (2016, September 28).

Lord-Mallam, N. (2012). *The Politics of the United Nations Security Council Reform Paperback.* Latvia: LAP Lambert Academic Publishing.

Luck, E. (2006). *UN Security Council: Practise & Promises.* New Delhi: Publisher Routledge, 2006.

Lynch, C. (2020, March 27)." UN Security Council Paralyzed as Contagion Rages". *Foreign policy Magzine.*

Mangone, G. J. (1954). *A Short History of International Organisation,.* New York:, Mc Graw Hill,.

Mathur, P. (1964)." The role of India in United Nation". *The Indian Journal of Political Science,* 90-93.

Mehrish, B. (2007). *The United Nations in the New Millennium : A Changing Scenerio.* Delhi: Academic Excellence.

Menon, B. (1995, Feb 19). "New Round of Musical Chairs". *The Sunday Times of India.*

Menon, S. (2020). *India's Foreign Affairs Strategy,*Impact Series *052020-02.* Delhi: Brookings Institutions India Centre.

Mingst, M. P. (2010). *International Organizations,The Politics & Processes of Global Governance.* New Delhi: Viva Books.

Ministry of External Affairs of India. *http://www.mea.gov.in/Uploads/Publication Docs/.* (2015, June). Retrieved December 1, 2020 : http://www.mea.gov.in/Uploads/PublicationDocs/25009_External_Affairs_2014-2015__English_.pdf.

Modi, N. (2015, September 25). "Statement by Honorable Prime Minister Shri Narendra Modi(speech transcript)", The United Nations Summit for the Adoption of the Post-2015.

Mohanty, B. (2012). *Foreign Policy of India in the 21st Century.* New Delhi: New Century Publications.

Mohanty, B. (2017). *Foreign Policy of India in the 21 st century.* New Delhi: New Century Publications.

Moynihan, H. (2015). "Assessing the Legal Basis for UK Military Action in Syria."

Munshi, S.A. (2009). *The Intelligent Person Guide to Good Governance.* New Delhi: Sage Publications.

Murthy, C. (1995). "Making the UN Security Council More Representative: India's Prospects". *India in Tomorrow's United Nations.*

Murthy, C. (1995). India in Tomorrow's. In C. Murthy, *"Making the UN Security Council More Representative: India's Prospects* (p. 22). New Delhi.

Murthy, C. (2011). *India as a Non-permanent Member of the UN Security Council in 2011-12, Perspective.* Berlin: Berlin: Friedrich Ebert Stiftung.

Murthy, C. (2017, may 25)." UNSC: India's Membership and theRoad Ahead ". Retrieved november 27, 2020, from The Hindu: http://www.thehindu.com/ todays-paper/ tp-opinion/

Nadin, P. (2014, August 23). "Vision 2020: A Discussion of UN Security Council Reform". *Our World.*

Nadin, P. (2016). *UN Security Council Reform (Global Institutions).* Singapore: Publisher : Routledge; 1 edition (3 March 2016).

Nafed, A. (2005)." Permanent Membership in United Nation Security Council: India Diplomatic Initiative & Strategies". *India Quarterly, Vol.61, issue 4,* p. 1.

Nafey, A. (2005). "Permanent Membership in the UNSC: India's Diplomatic Initiatives and Strategies ". India Quarterly.

Natalino, P. N. (2013). "The European Union and the Reform of the UN Security Council:Toward a New Regionalism?".

Nations (2020). *https://www.un.org/securitycouncil/content/functions-and-powers.* Retrieved December 12, 2020, from United Nations: https://www.un.org/ securitycouncil/content/functions-and-powers

Nations, U. *Charter chapter 18, article 109, par 3.* New York.

Neslen, A. (2015, november 30). "India Unveils Global Solar Alliance of 120 Countries at Paris". *The Guardian.*

Online, F. (2019, October 12). "Big Snub to Pakistan! China did not raise Kashmir Issue during Modi-Xi talks in Mamallapuram". *Financial Express.*

Oudraat, C. d. (2000). "Intervention in Internal Conicts: Legal and Political Conundrums". *Carnegie Endowment for International Peace. Global Policy Program.*

P. Saksena, K. (1993). *Reforming the United Nations The Challenge of Relevance.* California: Sage Publications.

Padelford, N. (1948). "The Use of the Veto". *International organization.*

Padmanabhan, G. S. (2004). *The Writing on the Wall India Checkmates America 2017.* New delhi: Manas Publications.

Parker, C. (2019, August 13). "India's Clampdown on Kashmir Continues. Here's what you need to know". *The Washington Post.*

Pease, K. K. S. (2012). *International Organizations.* London: Routledge.

Permanent Mission of India(2016)."71st Session 2016 UN General Assembly: Background and Approach". New York, USA.

PIB. (2020). "Text of Prime Minister Address at G 20 ". Delhi: Prime Minister Office.

Pramit Pal Chaudhary, F. A. (2020, September 18). "75 years of UN- Need for Reforms" Rajya Sabha Channel. (V. Dahiya, Interviewer)

Press TV (2019, August 7). "Iran urges India, Pakistan to Resort to 'Dialogue, Peaceful Methods' Amid Kashmir Tensions". (2019, August 7). *Press TV.*

PTI. (2017, July 18). "Committed to Non-Discriminatory". *Economic Times.*

PTI. (2019, August 6). "Article 370". *India Today.*

PTI. (2019, June 26)." Asia Pacific Group Endorses India's Candidature for UNSC Non Permanent Seats". *Business Lines.*

PTI. (2019, October 18). "Ahead of Xi Jinping's Visit, China says Kashmir Issue Should Be Resolved Bilaterally". *The Economic Times.*

PTI. (2020, June 18). "India Elected Non Permanent Member of UN Security Council". *The Print.*

Rajagopalan, R. (2015). "Multilateralism in India's Nuclear Policy". In a. S. C Raja Mohan, *The Oxford Handbook of Indian Foreign Policy.*

Report, C.D.M. (2016). "Non-Consenus Decision-Making in the Security Council: an Abridged History" *Security Council Report.*

Res, G. (1963). "The United Nations". New York. Retrieved January, 2020 from https://www.globalpolicy.org/security-council/sanctions.html.

Retrieved March, 2020 from www.un.org.

Retrieved November 10, 2020, from https://www.un.org/securitycouncil/content/functions-and-powers.

Retrieved November, 2020, from https://www.google.co.in/search?source=hp&ei=Ec2jX822AvC-3LUP4cOl0Ao&q=global+ governance+ meaning&oq=global+ Governance&gs_ lcp=CgZwc3ktYWIQAR gDMgUIABDJAzIFCAAQs.

Retrieved October, 2020 from unite.un.org.

Retrieved September,2019 from https://www.nationsencyclopedia.com/United-Nations/The-Security-Council—.html.

Rich, L. M. (1969). *Charter of the United Nations.* New York: Colcombia University Press.

Roche, E. (2019, August 16). "At UNSC, China and Pakistan Fail to Censure India over Article 370". *Livemint.*

Roche, E. (2020, September 23)." India,three other Nations call for UN Security Council Revamp". *mint.e paper.*

Rohan Mukherjee, D. M. (2013, July 20). "India & the UN Security Council : An Ambiguous Tale". *Economic & Political weekly.*

Roy, S. (2021, January 14). *Indian Express.*

S.J.R. Bilgrami. (2004). *Dynamics of Sanctions in World Affairs.* New Delhi: Atlantic Publishers & Distributors.

Saksena, K. (1993). *Reforming the United Nations The Challenge of Relevance.* California: Sage Publications.

Saran, S. (2020,March 18)."India and Multilateralism" *The Hindu.*

Saxena, S. (2020, September 16). "IBSA calls for Speedy Global Efforts to Reform UN Security Council". *Hindustan Times.*

Schaffer, T. C. (2010). "India: Driving the Global Superhighway". *The Brown Journal of World Affairs,* Volume XVI, Issue II.

Science, I. C. (2020). *UN Announces List of Countries for Working Group on Sustainable Development Goals.* Retrieved November 30, 2020, from ICSU: http://www.icsu.org/news-centre/news/un-announces-list-of-countries-for-working-groupon-sustainable-development-goals

Security Council Report (2020). *Security Council.*

Sen, S. (1996). *United Nations & the Global Challenge.* New Delhi: Kanishka Publishers Distributors.

Shivam, R. K. (2017). *India's Foreign Policy Nehru to Vajpayee.* Delhi: Arjun Publishing House.

Shivam, R. K. (2017). *India's Foreign Policy Nehru to Vajpayee.* New Delhi: Commonwealth Publishers.

Simma, B.S.P. (2002). "Article 27—Voting. In The Charter of the United Nations: A commentary". *The Charter of the United Nations: A commentary.*

Singh, M. (2018). *India's Relation with South Asian Countries.* New Delhi: The Readers Paradise.

Singh, S. "China's Kashmir Policy,". *World Affairs 16, no. 2 (April–June 2012): 102.*

Singh, S.K. (2017). *India's Foreign Policy Continuity with difference under MODI Government.* New Delhi: Manak Publications pvt.Ltd.

Singh, S.K. (2017). *India's Foreign Policy.* New Delhi : Manak Publications.

Sinha, R.K.. (2004). *India 2025,Social,Economic & Political Stability.* New Delhi: Shipra Publications.

Sreeram, C. (2009). *India and United Nations,Hand book of India's International Relations.* New York and London: Edited by Scott David, Routlege (Taylor and Francis group).

Statement, F. T. (2017, June 2)." Full Text of G4 Joint Statement". *The Times of India 2015.*

Stephen, C. (2001). *India: Emerging Power.* Brookings.

Stephen, S. (1997). "Can the United Nations Reform?" *World Policy Journal.*

Subramanian, A. (2015, May 13). "Green Road to Paris". *The Indian Express.*

Subramanian, N. (2015, November 17). "Global Anti-Terror Compact: Why India Wants One Where It Is Stuck". *The Indian Express.*

Talukdar, S. (2020, May 8). "India's Walked a fine Foreign Policy line during COVID-19 Crisis; Test ahead lies in how Modi handles Big Powers". *First Post.*

The Economic Times (2019, August 6) "Article 370: US Urges all Stakeholders to Maintain Peace, Stability along LoC".

The Hindu (2019, June 28)."At the high table: on India's Non-Permanent seat at UNSC".

The Hindu (2020, April 29). "India Permanent seat in UNSC".

The Hindu (2020, October 13).

The Hindu (2021, January 28).

The Times of India (2015, June 2). "G4 Joint Statement".

The Tribune (2020, December 27). "India will be 5th Largest economy in 2025, 3rd by 2030: UK Think Tank".

The Wire (2020, june 18). "India Elected for the 8th term as Non-Permanent UNSC Member".

Times, E. (2020, May 23)." Dr Harsh Vardhan elected as WHO's Executive Board Chairman". *Health World.com.*

UN, P. M. (2020). *https://www.pminewyork.org/pages.php?id=1987.* Retrieved December 1, 2020, from "India and the United Nations -Counter-Terrorism," Permanent Mission of India to the United Nations: https://www.pminewyork.org/pages.php?id=1987.

United Nations (2017, May 1). *https://www.un.org/sg/en/content/sg/statement/2005-01-28/secretary-generals-public-lecture-india-international-centre-larger.* Retrieved December 5, 2020, from United Nations: 28/secretary- generals-public-lecture-india-international-centre-larger

United Nations (2020)https://www.un.org/en/sections/un-charter/chapter-v/index.html. Retrieved 12.11, 2020, from United Nations: ttps://www.un.org/en/sections/un-charter/chapter-v/index.html

Webster, C. (1933). *The League of Nations in Theory and Practice.* London: George Allen

World BANK. "World development Indicators".

Worsnip, B.P. (2009, February 19). Reuter. *UN launches Talk to Expand Security Council.*

Yadav, M.K. (2014)." India's Quest for United Nations Security Council". *International journal of Humanities & Social Science.*

York, P.M. (2014, April 23). "Joint G4 Statement delivered by Amb. Asoke Mukerji". *Permanent Mission of India in New York.*

Zhenqiang, P. (2005). "On Reforms of the UN Security Council". *Online Info-Service Vol. 2/2005*

Chapter - 5

Concluding Remarks

The United Nations as a global diplomatic and political organization arose on the ashes of the League of Nations that was created by the Treaty of Versailles in 1919 and disbanded in 1946. The United Nations charter was signed on June 26, 1945 in San Francisco at the conclusion of United Nations Conference on International Organization. The charter came into force on October 24, 1945. It consists a preamble and 19 chapters divided into 111 articles. Initially UN had only 51 members with the addition of South Sudan in 2011, there are 193 members of United Nations plus two non-member countries with permanent observer states, The Vatican and The State of Palestine. As of 26th February 2021, UNSC has passed 2565 resolutions. Resolutions of UNSC are also vetoed by permanent members of Security Council 293 times vetoes have been used by Security Council.

Countries those have sanctions placed on them includes Angola, Burundi, Ethiopia and Eritrea, Iran, Iraq, Ivory Coast, Liberia, Libya, Nigeria, North Korea, Rwanda, Sierra Leone, Somalia, Sudan and the Former Yugoslavia. Each of these sanction regimes have been followed by Global Policy Forum. Although Nobel Prize for Peace was given to UN Peace Keeping Force in 1988, yet several of its missions invited criticism also. As of 30 June 2019, there are 100,411 people serving in UN peacekeeping operations (86,145 uniformed, 12,932 civilian, and 1,334 volunteers).

Weakening of the Security Council

India is among the many countries that are worried about the weakening of international institutions and the tendency to impose unilateral preferences over others. The Security Council needs to be reformed to correct some of the founding weaknesses in its composition and powers. India has argued since 1992 that the Security Council needs democratization in tune with the changed realities. Both changes of China and Russia took place without amendment in Charter, France and United Kingdom is no longer global powers. The US is the only permanent member that retains its original power but its commitment to multilateralism is doubtful. All permanent members have misused the veto power. China's commitment to democracy, Human Rights and peaceful settlement of disputes are totally smashed. It is the only country which is not party to International Covenant on Civil and Political Rights and refused to honour international arbitration in South China Sea dispute.

During Covid-19 pandemic the Security Council was paralyzed. Paralysis came at a time when United States was pressing a fifteen nation council to adopt a resolution for blaming China for spread of the Corona virus. The silence of UNSC under China's Presidency in March 2020 on the issue of human security reflected that it is not fit for handling the challenges.

India's Claim for Permanent Membership of the Security Council

India's justification for permanent seat of Security Council is, based on its contribution for world peace and security. India is among the largest troop contributors to UN Peacekeeping Missions. India has taken part in 44 peacekeeping missions with 180,000 troops. In the arena of peace keeping India is the largest contributor with 180,000 troops since 1950. Currently, around 7700 Indian peacekeepers have been deployed in 13 missions in 11 countries out of total 16 missions. India has lost more peacekeepers in the line of duty than any other UN member state and over the last 70 years, more than 160 Indian military, police and civilian personnel have lost their lives while serving in UN peacekeeping missions around the world.

To restore confidence in international cooperation and Global governance G4 nations in a virtual meet called for a revamp of the UN Security Council on 23 September,2020 to make it more representative, legitimate and effective of the current global order. Indian Government emphasised the need for expansion of the Security Council in both categories (permanent and non-permanent) to preserve its credibility and stopping it from becoming obsolete. G4 countries reiterated their support for each other's candidatures as aspiring new permanent members in reformed Security Council. Four Permanent members of UNSC support India i.e. Britain, France, Russia and the U.S. Only China is opposing. India.

Intended Benefit of Permanent Membership

Permanent seat in the UNSC would provide India with the much-needed leverage to expand its geo-political and geo-economic clout globally.

- Inclusion of India into UNSC will help in transforming its status from being a responsible stakeholder to a global rule-maker.
- Indian presence at the Security Council would ensure Indian interests are not sacrificed at the altar of great power politics.
- It would serve as an equalizer to China, its rival and an emerging hegemony in Asia and an ever-increasing strategic and security concern in its immediate neighbourhood and beyond.
- Most importantly, it will stall any possible intervention by China, a permanent member at the behest of its ally Pakistan.

Indian Claim to UNSC: The Challenges

Veto players are actors required for changing the status quo or conversely, without their consent, no institutional change is achievable. The configuration of veto players is set up by the constitutional provisions that give rise to the structure of an institution. Therefore, the prospect of successfully changing the status quo relies on the number of veto players and their preferences toward a new policy.

In order to change the size, composition, veto privileges and majority threshold applicable to the UNSC, notably to make it more representatives of current global power distributions, the UN Charter text of articles 23 and 27 would need to be amended. To achieve this, these provisions, like any other in the UN Charter could be altered by adopting a UNGA resolution (UN Charter art. 108) or by first convening a "General Conference" of all UN Members "for the purpose of reviewing the present Charter," which then could recommend an "alteration" of the Charter text corresponding to a UNGA resolution (UN Charter art. 109). In essence, both provisions require a comprehensive formal agreement by a two-thirds majority and subsequent ratification by two-thirds of the UNGA, as well as the permanent members of the UNSC. To date, however, the composition of the UNSC has been amended only once increasing its membership from 11 to 15 according to the provisions of Article 108, while Article 109 has never been applied.

With a total number of 193 member states, the two-thirds majority threshold in the UNGA (i.e. about 67 percent of total UNGA membership), amounts to 129 votes; accordingly, a blocking minority can be formed by 65 states (i.e. about 33 percent of the total).

Road Blocks in India's Path

- It is argued by critics that India has still not signed the NPT and also refused to sign the CTBT in 1996.
- China, which has veto power in the UNSC being one of its five permanent members, has been stonewalling India's efforts to become a permanent member.
- Though India is a bright spot in the global economy and its macroeconomic fundamentals are stable, yet it shows poor performance in many socio-economic indicators like the Human Development Index. Out of 189 countries, India has ranked 131 on Human Development Index 2020.
- India is competing with other countries of G4 grouping (Japan, Brazil and Germany) for a spot for permanent membership in UNSC.

- India's capacity to project its military power beyond the Indian Ocean region is still to be tested. Further, India heavily relies on weaponry imports from US and Russia for its military requirements.

Future Prospects

In order to meet realities of 21st Century the urgent need of reforms in United Nations Security Council is felt for a long time. No reforms of United Nations are complete without changing the composition of the Security Council.

The United Nations must have an efficient and capable bureaucracy, it must have the resources to carry on its work, and it must get past members pushing agendas solely on the basis of state interest. India can actively take the lead on the first two problems. It must commit to sending its best and brightest to serve in the international institution.

India must increase dramatically the amount of money it sends to support UN activities, must send forces and supporting materials to support UN missions, and must in other ways step up to assume a much greater share of the burden of maintaining this crucial international body. Altering the nature of representation at the UN is by far the trickiest element of change, but it is also the most critical. Only by becoming more responsive and representative will the international institution lives up to the dreams of its creators and the needs of our time. India that leads the way on human rights, climate control, and the fight against poverty and injustice, that assumes greater responsibility in and for the United Nations, that partners with the United States even as it partners with other countries around the world, and that tirelessly works to reform the UN will be an India that the world admires and respects. It will be at the forefront of the creation of a better tomorrow for all of earth's children.

Based on these credentials, India's claim for permanent membership is supported by G4 countries, majority of the permanent members of UNSC and the majority of countries in the United Nations General Assembly. Therefore, India's inclusion in UNSC will strengthen India's stature as a 'moralistic force' for the developing states and help in making UNSC more democratic. To strengthen UN system to combat new global challenges such as terrorism, piracy, disarmament, peace building, peace keeping and Human Rights India can play an effective role as a permanent member of the Security Council.

Thus, it can be concluded that on the basis of its population, territorial size, GDP, economic potential, civilization legacy, cultural diversity, political system and past and on-going contributions to the activities of the UN, especially to UN peacekeeping operations, India is eminently qualified for permanent membership.

Prime Minister Narender Modi while addressing to the High-Level meeting of the General Assembly to commemorate the 75th anniversary of the United Nations said.

"We cannot fight today's challenges without dated structures. Without comprehensive reforms, the UN faces a crisis of dignity. Time has come to retain lost credibility of Security Council through inclusion of India having 17 percent of population".

Reforms and reorganization of structure and processes of the Security Council are urgently required to regain its lost credibility and for inclusion in the permanent membership seat of Security Council, Indian tryst for permanent membership of Security Council is justified. As an undisputed leader of the Third World countries, India has been acknowledged as a rising power by the world. Time has come when the Security Council has to grow out of its five power mind-set to survive. India has to display more pragmatism to realize its aspiration to be a permanent member of the Security Council.

At UNSC, India pledged to be guided by the five priorities under the overreaching theme of Norms :New orientation for a reformed multilateral system. These are opportunities for progress, effective response to international terrorism, reforming multilateral systems, comprehensive approach to international peace and security and technology with a human touch. India will pursue these priorities through 5–S approach: Samman, Samvad, Sahyog, Shanti, and Samridhi.

When India is celebrating 75 years of India's independence inclusion of India as permanent member of Security Council will definitely add to its celebration and it will be remembered as the year of pride and achievement. India's optimism will be able to swing for itself a permanent seat in United Nations Security Council.

Bibliography

Books

Abbi, R. (2017). *United Nations Organization:Its Role in Third World Countries.* New Delhi:The Readers Paradise.

Allain, Jean. (2008). *The Slavery Conventions: The Travaux Préparatoires of the 1926 League of Nations Convention and the 1956 United Nations Convention.* USA: Martinus Nijhoff Publishers.

Aslund, Anders; Sergei Guriev, Andrew Kuchins (ed). (2010) *Russia After the Global Economic Crisis*, Washington, DC: Columbia University Press.

Batra, T. S. (1979). *The Security Council & Veto.* Delhi: B.V.Gupta Publishers.

Bhola, P. (2001). *Foreign Policies of India,Pakistan & China.* Delhi: RBSA Publishers.

Bhola, P. (2001). *Foreign Policies of India,Pakistan & China.* Jaipur: RBSA Publishers.

Bilgrami, S. J. (2004). *Dynamics of Sanctions in World Affairs.* New Delhi : Atlantic Publishers & Distributors.

Boulden, Jane; Ramesh Chandra Thakur, Thomas George Weiss (2009) *The United Nations and Nuclear Orders.* USA: United Nations University Press.

C.K. Webster. (1933). *The League of Nations in Theory and Practice.* London : George Allen and Unwin Ltd.

Duane, S. (2002). *Global Capital,Political Institutions & Policy Changes in Developed Welfare States.* Cambridge,U.K.: Cambridge University Press.

Genser, Jared; Bruno Stagno Ugarte (2014) *The United Nations Security Council in the Age of Human Rights.* New York: Cambridge University Press.

Hayes, Subside; Kiho Yi (2015) *Multifaceted Nature, Security and Civil society in East Asia: Foreign policies and the Korean Peninsula.* UK: Open Book Publishers.

Hening, Ruth *(2010). The League of Nations Makers of the Modern World.* London: Haus Publishing.

J. Padelford, N. (1948). *The Use of the Veto in International Organization,* Cambridge,U.K.: Cambridge University Press.

Kelly-Kate. (2012). *International Organization Fifth Edition.* London: Taylor & Francis Group.

Korbel, Josef (2015) *Risk in Kashmir.* USA: Princeton University Press.

Lord-Mallam, N. (2012). *The Politics of the United Nations Security Council Reform Paperback.* Latvia: Lambert Academic Publishing.

Lowe, Vaughan; Adam Roberts and Jennifer Welsh (2010) *The United Nations Security Council and War: The Evolution of Thought and Practice since 1945.* UK: Oxford University Press.

Luck, E. (2006). *UN Security Council: Practise & Promises.* New Delhi: Publisher Routledge.

Maaroof, Mohammad Khalid (1990) *United Nations and Afghanistan Emergency.* New Delhi: Commonwealth Publishers.

Mangone, G. J. (1954). *A Short History of International Organisation.* New York: Mc Graw Hill,.

Mehrish, B. (2007). *The United Nations in the New Millennium : A Changing Scenerio.* Delhi: Academic excellence.

Menon, S. (2020). *India's Foreign Affairs Strategy,Impact Series* 05-2020-02. Delhi: Brookings Institutions India Centre.

M*ingst, M. P. (2010). International Organizations, The Politics & Processes of Global Governance. New Delhi: Viva Books.*

Mohanty, B. (2012). *Foreign Policy of India in the 21st Century.* New Delhi: New Century Publications.

Munshi, S. A. (2009). *The Intelligent Person Guide to Good Governance.* New Delhi: Sage Publications.

Murthy, C. (1995). *Making the UN Security Council More Representative: India's Prospects.* India in Tomorrow's United Nations. Berlin: Berlin: Friedrich Ebert Stiftung.

Murthy, C. (2011). *India as a Non-permanent Member of the UN Security Council in 2011-12, Perspective.* Berlin: Berlin: Friedrich Ebert Stiftung.

Nadin, P. (2016). (*UN Security Council Reform Global Institutions*). Singapore: Routledge Publishers.

P.Saksena, K. (1993). *Reforming the United Nations The Challenge of Relevance.* California: Sage Publications.

Padmanabhan, G. S. (2004). *The Writing on the Wall India Checkmates America* 2017. New Delhi: Manas Publications.

Pease, K.K.S. (2012). *International Organizations.* London: Routledge Publishers

R.S. (2004). *India 2025,Social,Economic & Political Stability.* New Delhi: Shipra Publications.

S.K. (2017). *India's Foreign Policy Continuity with Difference under MODI Government.* New Delhi: Manak Publications pvt.Ltd.

Sen, S. (1996). *United Nations & the Global Challenge.* New Delhi: Kanishka Publishers.

Shivam, R. K. (2017). *India's Foreign Policy Nehru to Vajpayee.* Delhi: Arjun Publishing House.

Singh, M. (2018). *India's Relation with South Asian Countries.* New Delhi: The Readers Paradise.

Stephen, C. (2001). *India: Emerging Power.* Washington, D.C: BrookingsInstitution Press

Webster, C. (1933). *The League of Nations in Theory and Practice,.* London: George Allen.

Wet, Erika de (2004) *The Chapter VII Powers of the United Nations Security Council.* USA: Hart Publishing.

Journals and Periodicals

Civil Service Chronicle (2021, January)."UN Adopts India Sponsored Resolutions on Nuclear Disarmment".

Davydov, A. (2020). "China,USA,Russia: Geopolitics and Pandemic". *Far Eastern Affairs is a Quarterly Journal of the Institute for Far Eastern Studies Issue 2,*

Gulati, S., Pal, A., & Bansal, A. (2020)." Fuzzy Evaluation of Impact of Lockdown Amid Corona Virus on Delhi's Pollution". *Advances in Mathematics: Scientific Journal.*

Kapstein, E. B. (2000). "Winners & Losers in Indian Economy". *International Organizations, Vol.54,No.2,Spring.*

Keohane, R. O. (2014). "Multilateralism: An Agenda for Research". *International NO 45,* No. 4 (Fall 1990): 731-46.

Khan, S. A. (2015, August 14). "Why India Deserves a Fixed UN Security Council Seat". *Politics.*

Kohli, A. (2006). "Politics of Economic Growth in India 1980-2005 -Part II: The 1990 & Beyond". *Economic & Political weekly,*

Lattila, V. (2019, May 28). "A New Proposal For UN Security Council Reform". *Oxford Research Group,*

Lavanya, R. (1995). "Democratization of the United Nation".. *Economic and Political Weekly,.* New york.

Mathur, P. (1964). "The Role of India in United Nation". *The Indian Journal of Political Science*, 90-93.

Nadin, P. (2014, August 23). "Vision 2020: A Discussion of UN Security Council Reform". *Our World.*

Nafed, A. (2005). "Permanent Membership in United Nation Security Council: India Diplomatic Initiative & Strategies". *India Quarterly, Vol.61, Issue 4.*

Permanent Mission of India."71st Session 2016, UN General Assembly: Background and Approach". (2016). New York, USA.

Rajagopalan, R. (2015). "Multilateralism in India's Nuclear Policy". In a. S. C Raja Mohan, *The Oxford Handbook of Indian Foreign Policy.*

Rohan Mukherjee, D. M. (2013, July 20). "India & the UN Security Council : An Ambiguous Tale". *Economic & Political weekly.*

Schaffer, T. C. (2010). "India: Driving the Global Superhighway". *The Brown Journal of World Affairs*, Volume XVI, Issue II.

Stephen, S. (1997). "Can the United Nations Reform?". *World Policy Journal.*

Zhenqiang, P. (2005). "On Reforms of the UN Security Council". *Online Info-Service Vol. 2/2005.*

News Papers

Ananthakrishnan, G. (2015, DECEMBER 9). "BASIC Optimistic About Legally Binding Paris Deal". *The HINDU.*

G4 Joint Statement. (2015, June 2). *The Times of India.*

Ghosh, P. (2020, November 17). "Terrorism, Covid-19 Vaccine, Self-Reliant India: What PM Modi said at 12th BRICS summit 2020". *Hindustan Times.*

Harsh.V.Pant, H. S. (2020, September 18). "75 years of UN-Need for Reforms" In Rajya Sabha Channel. (V. Dahiya, Interviewer)

Herzog, S. (1999). "Globalization & Povert Allevation in India". *Liberal Times.*

Indian Express. (2020, September 22). 'UN and the New Multilateralism ".

Jayaraman, T. (2009, November 26). "India's Strategy at Copenhagen". *The Hindu.*

Joshi, M. (2020, November 10). "Biden's China Policy". *The Tribune.*

Katju, V. (2015, JAN 31). "Working of External Affairs Ministry needs much Reform". *The Economic Times.*

Kazmin, A. (2009, DECEMBER 22). "India Welcomes Copenhagen Accord". *Financial Times.*

Krishnan, V. B. (2019, January 12). "India has Lost Highest Number of Personnel in UN Peacekeeping Mission". *The Hindu.*

Leveringhaus, K. S. (2017, June 30). "China's Stance on NSG Membership shows the Extent of India's Challenge in the Global Nuclear Order". *The Wire.*

Lewis, P. (1997, March 21)." U.N.Panel Proposes Expanding Security Council to 24 Members". *The NewYork Times.*

Livemint. (2012). "What Is the Comprehensive".

Livemint. (2016, September 28). "What Is the Comprehensive Convention on International Terrorism ?".

Menon, B. (1995, Feb 19)." New Round of Musical Chairs".

Modi, N. (2015, September 25). "Statement by Honorable Prime Minister Shri Narendra Modi(speech transcript, The United Nations Summit for the Adoption of the Post-2015)".

Neslen, A. (2015, November 30). "India Unveils Global Solar Alliance of 120 Countries at Paris". *The Guardian.*

PIB. (2020). "Text of Prime Minister Address at G 20". Delhi: Prime Minister Office.

Pramit Pal Chaudhary, F. A. (2020, September 18). "75 years of UN- Need for Reforms"Rajya Sabha Channel (V. Dahiya, Interviewer).

Roche, E. (2020, September 23)." India,three other Nations Call for UN Security Council Revamp". *mint.e paper.*

Saxena, S. (2020, September 16). "IBSA calls for Speedy Global Efforts to Reform UN Security Council". *Hindustan Times.*

Statement, F. T. (2017, June 2). "Full Text of G4 Joint Statement". *The Times of India 2015.*

Subramanian, A. (2015, MAY 13). "Green Road to Paris". *The Indian Express.*

Subramanian, N. (2015, November 17). "Global Anti-Terror Compact: Why India wants One where it is Stuck,". *The Indian Express.*

Talukdar, S. (2020, May 8). "India's walked a fine Foreign Policy line during COVID-19 Crisis; Test ahead lies in how Modi handles Big Powers". *First Post.*

The Hindu. (2020, October 13). *The Hindu.*

The Tribune (2020, December 27). "India will be 5th Largest Economy in 2025,3rd by 2030:UK Think Tank".

Worsnip, B. P. (2009, February 19). Reuter." UN Launches Talk to Expand Security Council".

York, P. M. (2014, April 23). "Joint G4 Statement Delivered by Amb. Asoke Mukerji". *Permanent Mission of India in New York.* Retrieved from Permanent Mission of India in New York.

Websites

Bussemaker, N. (2020, september 16). *https://www.cfr.org/backgrounder/un-security-council.*

Das, D. (2016, June 10). *http://www.catchnews.com/international-news/india-smembership-in-the-nsg-is-symbolic-lack-of-success-does-it-no-harm-1465552409.html.*

ExternalAffair(December2015).http://www.mea.gov.in/Uploads/PublicationDocs/25009

Freiesleben, J.V. (2020, November 20). *Reforms in Security Council.* Retrieved from https://www.globalpolicy.org/images/pdfs/032008reform.pdf.

Freiesleben,J.V.(2020, November 20). *Reforms in Security Council.* Retrieved from https://www.globalpolicy.org/images/pdfs/032008reform.pdf.

Freiesleben,J.V.(2020, November 20). *Reforms in Security Council.* Retrieved from https://www.globalpolicy.org/images/pdfs/032008reform.pdf.

General, R. O. (2005). *'In larger freedom: towards development, security and human rights for all.* http://www.globalpolicy.org/images/pdfs/followupreport.pdf.

General, U.N. (2017, May 1). *https://www.un.org/sg/en/content/sg/statement/2005-04-28/secretary- generals-public-lecture-india-international-centre-larger.*

Ghoshal, D.(2018, Feb 3). *https://scroll.in/article/867260/while-no-one-was-watching-india-worked-to-position-itself-as-a-responsible-nuclear-powered-nation.*Retrievedfrom Scroll: https://scroll.in/article/867260/while-no-one-was-watching-india-worked-to-position-itself-as-a-responsible-nuclear-powered-nation.

Harder,A.(2017, june 1). *https://www.wilsoncenter.org/publication/not-the-cost-china-india-and-the-united-nations-security-council-1950.* Retrieved from unsc: https://www.wilsoncenter.org/publication/not-the-cost-china-india-and-the-united-nations-security-council-1950

http://www.mea.gov.in/Uploads/PublicationDocs/25009_External_Affairs_2014-2015__English_.pdf.

https://www.cfr.org/backgrounder/four-nuclear-outlier-states

https://www.cfr.org/backgrounder/un-security-council

https://www.globalpolicy.org/security-council/index-of-countries-on-the-security-council-agenda/sanctions.html.

https://www.indiatoday.in.

https://www.un.org/en/sections/un-charter/chapter-v/index.html.

https://www.un.org/securitycouncil/content/functions-and-powers.

https://www.www.un.org.

India, M.O. (Annual Report: 2014-2015, 170, Annual Report: 2014-2015, 170 Annual Report: 2014-2015, 170). *http://www.mea.gov.in/Uploads/PublicationDocs/ 25009_* https://www.nationsencyclopedia.com/United-Nations/The-Security-Council

Ministry of External Affair (2015). http://www.mea.gov.in/Uploads/PublicationDocs/ 26525_26525_ External_Affairs_ English_AR_ 2015-16_Final_compressed.pdf. Retrieved December 1, 2020, from Ministry of External Affairs of India: http://www.mea.gov.in/Uploads/PublicationDocs/ 26525_26525_External_ Affairs_ English_ AR_ 2015-16_Final_compressed.pdf.

Murthy, C. (2017, may 25). *UNSC: India's membership and the road ahead.* Retrieved november 27, 2020, from The Hindu: http://www.thehindu.com/todays-paper/tp-opinion/www.indiatoday.in

Nations, P. M. *https://www.pminewyork.org/pages.php?id=1987.* Retrieved December 1, 2020, from "India and the United Nations -Counter-Terrorism," Permanent Mission of India to the United Nations: https://www.pminewyork.org/ pages.php?id=1987.